To the Town that Bears Your Name

A Young Woman's Journey to Nordegg in 1912

For

Anthony Joseph

Martin Nordegg

W. J. Koch

Edmonton, Canada

September 1996

Translated by Maria Koch
Commentary by W. John Koch

Brightest Pebble
Publishing Co. Inc.
1995

To Mrs. Martha Froelich

First Printing, October 1995 by:
Art Design Printing Inc., Edmonton Alberta, Canada

Cover design by Art Design

First published in 1995 by
Brightest Pebble Publishing Co. Ltd.
7604 - 149 Avenue
Edmonton, Alberta, Canada
T5C 2V7
Phone (403) 457-7496   Fax (403) 475-0243

Canadian Cataloguing in Publication Data

Nordegg, Martin, 1868-1948

To the Town that Bears Your Name:
A Young Woman's Journey to Nordegg in 1912

ISBN 0-9699669-1-1

1. Nordegg, Martin, 1868-1948—Journeys—Canada.
2. Nordegg, Marcelle—Journeys—Canada.
3. Canada—Description and travel.
4. Canada—History—20th century.
5. Nordegg (Alta.)—Description and travel.
6. Nordegg (Alta.)—History.
I. Koch, W. John
II. Title.

FC74.N67 1995   917.104'612   C95-900949-3
F1015.N59 1995

Illustration on cover "Main Street Nordegg, Alberta - 1957" by Serena Duncan ©

Table of Contents

The production of this book
was funded in part by the
ALBERTA HISTORICAL
RESOURCES FOUNDATION

ACKNOWLEDGEMENTS

It is not without significance that both Maria and John grew up in mining areas of Germany, Maria in the Ore Mountains of Saxony near the "Silver Trail" famous in centuries past, and John in the coal mining district of Lower Silesia, only a stone's throw from the town where Martin Nordegg was born in 1868. Perhaps, Maria's and John's lifelong fascination with the history of various mining ventures in Germany and in Canada can be traced to their childhood years.

Historical and social aspects of coal mining in Lower Silesia were already part of John's earlier publications. More recently, this particular interest led to John's work on the biography of Martin Nordegg which is currently in progress. Good fortune, persistence and imagination, but foremost patience made the research on Martin Nordegg's life — much of it previously so enigmatic — successful. Success, however, would have remained elusive, had it not been for the good will, interest and support of so many persons, archives and other public and private resources in Canada, the United States and several European countries too numerous to name at this time. Since their help was and is primarily intended to assist John in the completion of Martin Nordegg's biography, their contributions will be gratefully acknowledged in the Martin Nordegg biography at the time of its publication. At this time, however, Maria and John wish to express their appreciation for the interest and assistance instrumental in the translation of Martin Nordegg's story *To the Town that Bears Your Name,* and its publication to the following:

Maria and John are deeply grateful to the friend of the late Mrs. Sonia Nordegg, Mrs. Martha Froelich of New York City. Without Mrs. Froelich's interest and support, the publication of this story would not have been possible.

With his thoughtful and informative commentaries and footnotes accompanying his edited version of Martin Nordegg's memoirs *The Possibilities of Canada Are Truly Great,* published by MacMillan of Canada in 1976, Professor T.D. Regehr of Saskatoon, Saskatchewan, greatly assisted John in the early stages of research.

With never-ending patience and resourcefulness, Ms. Diane Duguay of the National Archives of Canada opened many doors to the history of Martin Nordegg's life.

Mr. Hyman Mizell of Miami, Florida and the late Mrs. Ruth Rothchild of Tampa, Florida and members of their families shared many personal reminiscences and papers of Martin and Sonia Nordegg with Maria and John.

Mr. Fred Kidd of Cochrane, Alberta, son of Stuart Kidd who accompanied Martin Nordegg and his daughter Marcelle on their trip on horseback across the Rockies in 1912, and Mrs. Virginia Kidd of Edmonton, Alberta, wife of the late George Kidd, son of Stuart Kidd, made their rich memories and important documents available to Maria and John.

Anne Belliveau, John Galloway, Joe Baker and other members of the Nordegg Historical Society helped with advice and resources.

Allan and Kathy Shute of Edmonton gave Maria and John inspiration and much encouragement over the past years.

Maria and John thank their son George for his editorial and technical advice.

Maria and John express their gratitude to Mr. James Musson, Brightest Pebble Publishing Company, Ltd., Edmonton, Alberta for his courage and his decision to publish Martin Nordegg's story.

INTRODUCTION

This is the story Martin Nordegg wrote for his daughter Marcelle after their journey across his beloved Canada in the late summer and early fall of 1912. While researching the life of Martin Nordegg,* John Koch came across this story flawlessly typed by Martin and complemented by a number of photographs taken by him. The typed sheets were bound in a leather cover adorned with a Western motif. Written in excellent German prose reflecting Martin's classical education, the account of his journey with Marcelle was translated into English by Maria Koch to make this piece of early Alberta history accessible to those interested in the development of the province, in its people, and in its beautiful nature; to those already familiar with the Nordegg country; to others who, after reading Martin's story from 1912, might feel intrigued to explore the present site of the former town and mine of Nordegg, which was so much Martin's creation and the realization of his dreams. The story was translated for those whose parents or grandparents played a part in Martin's life and his introduction to the Canadian West; and for former Nordegg residents, who have remained interested in Martin's life and personality.

Martin was born in 1868 in Reichenbach, Germany in the Province of Silesia, where he received a high school education of the classical-hu-

---

* Martin Nordegg will hereafter be referred to by his first name rather than his last so as not to confuse Nordegg the man with Nordegg the town.

manistic type. Following his army service, Martin attended the Technical Institute which later became the Technical University of Berlin. He specialized in the fields of engineering and photochemistry. Employed by one of Germany's foremost printing plants, Martin spent several years in England and Ireland, where his skills in English and photography advanced considerably. While living in London, he married a French woman in 1897. It was also in London that his only child, his daughter Marcelle, was born in 1898.

After his return to Berlin, Martin became the manager of Berlin's largest printing plant, renowned for its multi-colour printing process that had been developed in the laboratories of the Berlin Technical Institute where Martin continued to work part-time. In 1905, while at work in his laboratory, Martin was introduced to a visitor from Canada. His name was Colonel Talbot, a Member of Parliament in Ottawa. He was so impressed with Martin's personality and skills that he urged the young man to try his luck in Canada. Supported by his employer, Georg Büxenstein, a man of remarkable entrepreneurial skill and spirit, who founded the "German Canadian Development Corporation," Martin arrived as its representative in New York on May 6, 1906, and proceeded immediately to Ottawa. His French-born wife Berthe-Marie and his seven-year old daughter Marcelle remained in Germany.

Martin quickly became an entrepreneur who recognized opportunities and responded to the challenges Canada offered to a man of his intelligence, energy and sense of adventure. He readily succeeded in capturing the interest and support of Sir Wilfrid

Laurier and other political figures in Ottawa. Moreover, he liked the country and its people and fell in love with the beauty and vastness of the Canadian wilderness.

After searching with little success for opportunities in the mining country of Northern Ontario which was still gripped by the silver boom near Cobalt, Martin turned his attention to the Canadian West and its vast resources of coal, much in demand at a time when new railways were built throughout the Prairies and across the Rocky Mountains. Entering into a partnership with Sir William Mackenzie of the Canadian Northern Railway, Martin undertook several expeditions into the foothills country southwest of Edmonton and west of Calgary, exploring and staking coal fields in a number of locations.

By 1912, Martin was well established among the financial and business circles in the East and, as explorer and developer of the soon to be opened coal mines at Nordegg in the Canadian West. He learned to love the Rocky Mountains as much as Europe's Alps. It seemed time to introduce his daughter Marcelle to the country he felt part of by now and to his endeavours at Nordegg that were rapidly coming to fruition.

Once before, Martin had shown Marcelle a small part of Canada during an earlier, brief visit to Banff. In the meantime, Marcelle had attended Sacré Coeur Academy, a private school in New York City. In August 1912, Martin brought his fourteen-year old daughter to Toronto. From there, they began their journey across Canada by train, horse-drawn wagon, and finally by freightcar and caboose on the partly completed railroad to Rocky Mountain House. From there, they travelled on horseback to Nordegg and across the Pipestone Pass to Lake Louise. From Banff, their journey continued West by train ending at the Pacific Ocean in Victoria.

Only very few readers of this account of the travells of Martin Nordegg and his daughter Marcelle will be familiar with Martin Nordegg's memoirs of his Canadian years between 1906 and 1924, that demonstrate so eloquently his powers of observation and his writing skills, that are no less obvious in this earlier example of Martin Nordegg's writing dating back to 1912. In contrast to his memoirs, however, the story of the 1912 journey has a much more immediate character; it is written for a young person much loved by her father. The father's pride in his daughter, who mastered the challenges of this often strenuous trip so exceedingly well, shines throughout the pages of his story. But there is more to it than the memory of an unforgetable adventure embarked upon by father and daughter. Martin's account of this journey also presents a vivid picture of the Canadian West and a way of life that has already faded into history, as has the way in which Martin and others viewed their contemporaries.* The story also preserves the memory of some of Martin's loyal friends who accompanied him and Marcelle on different parts of their journey or met the two travellers at one point or another along the way.

Translating Martin's story was not an easy task. Written in a vivid, rapidly moving style, the story never becomes boring, even though Martin almost

---

* It is recognized that some of the expressions Martin used may not be appropriate today, but he never meant any ill will toward any human being.

obsessively takes note of every small detail and event observed or encountered. In his unique way, he adds one detail to the next in a seemingly never ending chain of images, creating a composite picture that comes to life in the mind of the reader, as if he or she would look at a photograph of the scene or scenery Martin describes. This, by the way, is easier done in German than in English. The German language lends itself well to connecting one image or observation to the next with the help of an "and" rather than the use of a participle, a semicolon or an entirely new sentence.

Obviously, a choice had to be made in translating Martin's story by either consistently using English syntax or by consciously preserving, wherever possible, the original German sentence structure in the effort to retain the vitality, charm and style of the original, which says so much about Martin Nordegg himself. It is hoped that the choice made after much deliberation will appeal to the reader as the best way to transmit as much as possible the character of the original German manuscript and its author's personality.

Maria and John Koch
Edmonton, Alberta, Canada
1995

Meiner geliebten Tochter Marcelle zur Erinnerung an die September-Tage 1912 in den Canadischen Rockies.

MEIN LIEBES KIND!

Nun bist Du vierzehn Jahre alt geworden und fähig, grosse Eindruecke in Dich aufzunehmen und fuer Dein ganzes Leben zu bewahren. Deshalb nahm ich Dich nach dem Westen Canadas mit und zeigte Dir dieses ungeheure Land, das erst im Anfang seiner Entwicklung steht. War ich mir einerseits bewusst, dass es auf den Phasen dieser langen und abwechslungsreichen Reise — im Pullmanwagen, im Güterwagen, schliesslich mit Cowboys und Indianern auf Gebirgspferden — mancher Entsagung und Entbehrung Deinerseits beduerfen wuerde, so war ich andererseits ueberzeugt davon, dass diese in Deiner Erinnerung verschwinden werden, und nur noch das Grosse und Schoene, das Du geschaut, Dlr unausloeschlich im Gedaechtnis bleiben wird.*

---

* From Martin Nordegg's original text.

I

My Dear Child:

Now that you have turned fourteen, you are capable of absorbing memorable impressions and retain them for your entire life. For this reason, I took you along to the Canadian West to show you this vast country that is only at the beginning of its development. On the one hand, I was aware that this would require some renunciation and privation on your part during the stages of this long and varied journey — in the Pullman, on the freight train and, finally, with cowboys and Indians on horseback. But, on the other hand, I was convinced these hardships would eventually fade from your memory and only the greatness and the beauty of what you had seen will remain in your memory forever.

On the last August night of 1912, we boarded the Vancouver Express of the Canadian Pacific Railway [in Toronto] which would house us for several days and nights. The big bell of the powerful locomotive began its shrill clanging, which would so often interrupt our sleep, alternating with the wolf-like dull howling of the steam whistle, and slowly the train began to move. While the black porter prepared our beds, I took you through the entire train, showed you the carriage for the immigrants with its varied smells, then the one with the somewhat better-off tourists, then the numerous elegant Pullman cars with the dining car in between and, finally, the observation car. You could see that the claim of running a one-class system is only a chimera and, in reality, three classes exist after all. Even in the "free" country of America, money makes a big difference when it comes to comfort and treatment while travelling.

Because of your joyous excitement about the impending journey and the unaccustomed environment, you did not find it easy to fall asleep but, finally, the constant rolling of the heavy cars lulled you to sleep, and we rushed past the beautiful Muskoka lake and forest area that, during the summer, is inhabited by families looking for relaxation and by mosquitoes feeding on them. When you awoke, we travelled through the rough and hilly country east of Lake Superior. On both sides of the track, blackened and

Marcelle on the observation platform

burnt tree stumps point sadly and bleakly into the sky like black exclamation marks. We also noticed the naked boulders, now and then interrupted by small groves of young deciduous trees through which the ever-active nature attempts re-forestation.

On this day and the days following, you liked to spend time in the observation car where, seated in comfortable chairs, one has an unobstructed view through the big windows, or you sat on the wide platform at the rear from where rain and dust often drove you away. In this uninhabited land, you rarely ever saw a house. More often you saw the wooden shacks that used to be inhabited by the railroad workers but had long since been abandoned. Every four or five hours, a "city" appeared which, in spite of its proud designation, could only show off a few wooden houses. These cities offered a welcome opportunity to stroll along the wooden platform. Sometimes, a further opportunity for a walk arose during an involuntary stop to let a train pass on the single track line. On such occasions you could prove your fishing skills when you tried to bait the non-existing fish in a pond. Then it turned evening again and the train that, during the day, carried us at an average speed of 45 kilometres [per hour] but stopped at every station, always became a fast train at night, stopping only at major stations. It was already dark when we travelled along the north shore of the huge Lake Superior and, at midnight, we passed through the twin cities of Port Arthur and Fort William.

When you awoke the next morning, we were already in the lovely area of the Lake of the Woods that ends near Kenora. Then, the last large forested area disappeared and rows of small hills gradually changed into the Prairie. Up to that point, we had not paid attention to our fellow-travellers, although you could not help speculating about them and their nationality, their looks, dress, behavior and their luggage. Most noticeable were the babies. Their number multiplied by the number of the two dozen transcontinental trains that were rolling daily across the country, presented you with a huge arithmetical problem the result of which was an optimistic picture of the future population of Canada. We got into closer contact with our fellow travelers while waiting for our seats in the dining car, which turned into more than an hour of standing at the door to the promised land in the crowded, drafty corridor! Hungry people are mostly in a bad mood, more so here, since even after reaching their goal, only a poorly prepared meal of inferior quality was waiting for them. While waiting, you looked into the kitchen and observed that a can-opener and stove were all the chef needed. The once shiny white of his uniform had long since turned into the colour of the cloth worn by the Black Hussars. During his hot activity, he often took a cool sip from a huge bottle.

Eventually, we reached the Prairie and I explained to you how much it resembles the Siberian Tundra in appearance, topography, soil conditions and climate; no more trees or shrubs, but endless, waving wheat fields reaching as far as the horizon. And finally, the ever more frequent appearance of better-looking houses signaled the proximity of a big city: first the wires of an electrical plant, then a highway alongside the railroad track, then the first house built of brick and, at last, the first electric streetcar.

And now, our porter appeared with his official strawbrush and brushed the dust off our clothes onto the already cleaned fellow travellers. This job was done with his right hand while his left stretched out expecting his "bak-sheesh" — called "tip" around here. Then his interest in us waned as fast as it had come. We were rolling into the large train-shed of the City of Winnipeg. I was lucky and succeeded in catching a red-capped lad who carried our hand luggage to the imposing Royal Alexandra Hotel owned by the Canadian Pacific Railway.

Although I had booked rooms two weeks before, more than forty names were on the waiting list ahead of us. What traffic! What else could we do but resign ourselves to our fate and decide to continue our trip the same evening?

While I hurriedly attended to my business calls, you sat in the luxurious lobby of the hotel watching the ever-changing flow of people passing by you. Later, I showed Winnipeg to you starting at the railroad station with its mixture of nationalities, where Scots and Hindus, Chinese and Slovaks, Italians, Greeks, Russians and Japanese sat peacefully next to each other guarding their belongings. Then, we took the streetcar which starts immediately at high speed and stops with a jolt so that the passengers are thrown back and forth. We drove through streets that seemed far too wide and were obviously planned for the future; we saw modern skyscrapers next to poor wooden shacks, a picture of the recent past and today's rapid progress. I told you that Winnipeg had not existed as recently as fifty years ago. It used to be

Fort Garry of the Hudson's Bay Company, that still operates a large department store in the city.

Just think, a few years ago only three log cabins enclosed by palisades, where the agent had often to defend himself against the Indians when he traded furs for guns, ammunition and whiskey. Then the "firewater" heated the heads of "nature's children" and the traded guns were now pointed at the vendor himself. And now, a big department store where the floor-walker receives you in a perfect tuxedo at the door!

Evening came. Again, we boarded the train and rolled towards the endless Prairie. You watched the wonderful sunset with its brilliant red colours around the clouds, which were flat and stretched out, so typical for the Great Plains; only near the Rocky Mountains would they resume their round shape.

The next morning, overripe wheat fields were swaying on both sides of the track, still waiting in vain for the harvesters. Then we reached the fallow areas that had not yet been sold because of land speculation or being too barren and arid. You were surprised to see hills now and then instead of a totally flat plain as you had envisioned the Prairie to be. The hills rose like terraces towards the West. With some effort you recognized the slowly fading tracks of the once huge herds of buffalo that have long been extinct, and you also discovered the deep ruts of the endless trail on which the first white settlers had "trekked" to the Far West.

At noon, we reached the station at Medicine Hat where the street lights burn day and night fed by natural gas, where Indian squaws of the Sarcees are sitting, offering their pearl and grass handicrafts, and where the splendid men of the North West Mounted Police patrol back and forth.

Near Crowfoot, you saw the big Blackfoot Indian Reserve rush by and at the next stop, Gleichen, I could already draw your attention to the zig-zag line of the Rocky Mountains at the farthest Western horizon. Then, along the railroad, the first canal of the large irrigation system of the Canadian Pacific Railway appeared, that had turned vast barren lands into fertile and inhabitable country. Finally, we arrived in Calgary where our friends warmly welcomed us.

The first message was quite depressing: a big festival was taking place here, and no rooms would be vacant in any hotel. We had no choice but to accept the hospitality of our acquaintances. The festival was a stampede where Indians and cowboys show their skills: taming horses that had never been ridden before, throwing lassoes, catching bulls and all sorts of riding expertise. Whiskey was flowing in torrents in the hotels and throughout the city, and, in the evening when we took a drive through the illuminated city with our friends, we saw a cowboy killed by a gunshot. He was lying in the street surrounded by a crowd of people.

The next afternoon, we met several of the engineers and the other people who would accompany us during the next days and weeks. There was the Belgian engineer who always had a huge appetite and could never quite satisfy it, then our outfitter Stuart Kidd. Born in Eastern Canada, Kidd had emigrated as a young man in search of adventure to the West where he had developed into a perfect cowboy. For years, he had been the agent of a trading post in

Morley, the reservation of the Stoney Indians, and knew their language. He was never happier than when he could outwit his Indians who were pretty cunning themselves.

A perfect horseman, hunter and mediator, always cheerful, willing and ready to work, he was, at the same time, also very well-read and an interesting conversationalist.

Finally, your special young friend Tom who, after graduating from the military academy, had been assigned to me to learn about business administration. He, too, had adventure in his blood and, once he left the office where he had been useless, he became indispensable. Wherever something had to be done, Tom was ready. Catching, saddling and packing horses, driving packtrains, pitching tents, gathering wood and splitting it, lighting the fire — Tom was always there and did everything to perfection. And when our newly hired cook did not appear at the time of our departure because he was totally drunk, Tom advanced to the cook's position. Poor Tom! You will never become a "Cordon Bleu" and we will forget about your shortcomings in culinary matters and cleanliness!

This was the company that was with us when we travelled north from Calgary to Edmonton.

With the delay usual for this country, we arrived at Strathcona, then the end of the train, and had to take the electric streetcar to be shaken about for three quarters of an hour to finally arrive in Edmonton after crossing the big bridge across the [North] Saskatchewan. That was your first encounter with "the river." You were wide-eyed when you saw the hotel in Edmonton, and your disappointment about the lack of any comfort left you speechless. You were so tired that, fortunately, you did not see all the things that had annoyed me for years. All you noticed were the men tired out by whiskey who were lying around in all kinds of contortions. Then God Morpheus took you in his arms and led you in your dreams to a clean room, I hope!

The next morning, there was much to do. First, all sorts of business matters had to be attended to, then provisions and equipment had to be checked, and in the afternoon we said farewell to semi-civilization by unpacking our belongings and distributing them on our beds. On one of the beds, there were the symbols of "the cultured," your blouses and dresses, white lingerie and shoes, my collars, dress shirts and ties. The other bed received the clothing of those people who go into the wilderness to be exposed to any kind of weather beyond good or evil: the big high boots, riding gaiters, leggings, heavy gloves, your woolen hat and my flat-topped riding hat, the heavy woolen underwear.

During those years of my pioneer life in Canada, I have learned to also divide all those little things that you think you might need into three piles: one for the things that you think you might need, the second for the items really needed and the third for the few objects without which you don't think you could survive. If one is sensible, one only takes the third pile and usually finds that even here, many useless things have crept in. This third pile finds room in a canvas bag that you throw over your shoulder and the traveller is ready!

Sorting your things was a struggle. You did not want to part with many items, and only later you may have recognized your errors that arose from your feminine vanity. You really did transport your mirror through the Rockies, but often you were wise not to look into it! Then we inspected the waterproof bags with the sleeping blankets and went to bed early.

The next morning we got up at 5:00 a.m. It was hardly daylight. Half asleep, we stumbled down the stairs and down the steep river bank to wait for the electric streetcar again.

Standing between the labourers and cowboys in an overcrowded streetcar and being thrown back and forth, were new experiences for the young lady from Sacré Coeur in New York. But your background could hardly be identified looking at the clothes you were wearing now. So for half an hour, we swayed back and forth like a grain field in the wind. Finally, even this torture passed and, till noon, we could rest in the Pullman car to Blackfalds in comfortable

Blackfalds

wicker chairs. Directly from the station, we went through the softest mud that gave the proper colour to our boots. Then, after a long wait in the proudly named Imperial Hotel, we devoured a few awful scraps and climbed into the springless carriage with whose grumbling driver I became friends with right away; two whiskeys and the conversation in his Habitant French helped us along.

Later, he not only became pleasant and amusing, but he also prognostigated that we would have to wait for hours and that the train would derail every so often, all of which made us incorrigible optimists only laugh more. How right he was, we unfortunately found out later and now, in hindsight, we look at him as a wise prophet.

Through deepest mud, we reached our destination on this part of our trip: a wooden water tower that, according to our driver and the railroad labourers we found hanging around, represented the station of the new Canadian Northern Western Railway. In the meantime, our freight wagon had arrived and, with the assistance of our slowly gathering crew, we unloaded our belongings, boxes and crates and began our travels with the one activity that from now on should become our most frequent and tiring one: Waiting! At this point, we discovered a sense of humour in the kitchen boy — he had just been hired for the coal mine — that would never fail him in future, even after it had long since turned into black humour. However, right now it helped us over a very boring hour. For any active person used to organizing his time systematically, there is no worse torture than standing around waiting uselessly.

Waiting

A brief stay in Western Canada, perhaps even a trip by train on a branch line or riding with a pack-train, will soon prove that time is of no concern whatever, except in regard to eating. However, I could not get used at all to this idle waiting and marched a few hundred yards along the tracks to the foreman of the big steam shovel. He was informed about everything except the only matter I was interested in, namely my question when our train would finally arrive. Consequently, I asked my way to the car where the crew was and, of course in the last one, I finally met a one-armed man who did know something. Even in this desolation, a message had reached him that the Vice President of the Canadian Northern Railway had booked a special train for us.

It should have arrived at noon, but since it was only 4:00 p.m. there was absolutely no reason to be alarmed.

Waiting again

Communication is handled by telephone rather than by telegraph, and after much shouting back and forth, the train actually arrived at 5:00 p.m. It consisted of a locomotive and tender, four freightcars and one caboose. The latter would house us longer than we cared for, so I think it is worth to refresh your memory. To begin with, one should not imagine anything better than a German cattle-car with the exception that the doors are at the rear and front rather than at the sides. On the roof at the rear of the caboose, there is a glassed-in dome with two loose boards at one side to lie or sit on. A desk and armchair are on the other side; below the dome are narrow cupboards for kitchen equipment and closets for coats. One gets to the dome by climbing from crossbar to crossbar like a chimney-sweep. Towards the center of the car, the narrow corridor opens to the full width of the caboose. First, there is the big iron stove and, across from it, the water barrel with a wash basin. In addition, there are four wide wooden benches covered with very thin woolen mattresses. That is all the furniture and equipment there is, except for a very smoky petroleum lamp.

The Canadian Northern Western on which the
Nordegg party travelled

When the train came to a halt, a father, a mother and their three daughters, four men and the engineer who at once introduced himself with innate intelligence, emerged from the caboose. He regretted very much that this was neither the special train nor would there be a special car for me. The "special" had derailed that morning, while this train was the regular weekly which should have arrived yesterday, but it had run into problems. I should travel with him. Otherwise, I would have to wait three more days. So, you and I climbed into the caboose. The engineers and the crew boarded one of the freightcars and, after some shrill clanging of the bell and whistling and hissing of the escaping steam, the train proudly began to move.

At the station (Marcelle and Martin at far right).

One of our cowboys had managed to get into the caboose with us, and I began to explain to him the modern achievements of the railroad compared to a packtrain. He constantly shook his head in disbelief while we were racing along at a speed of 8 km per hour on the admittedly very rough tracks. All our calculations as to the possible time of arrival were suddenly interrupted by a terrible bang. We were thrown against each other, pots and plates broke on the floor, and I believed it was an earthquake. Then, dead silence! We rushed outside where we sank ankle-deep into the rain-soaked mud, and then we stomped alongside the train. Only the coal-tender had jumped the tracks. After three hours of work, it was back on the tracks. We had used this stop to eat supper. You had your first experience of what such a picnic is like. A piece of canned American meat, a piece of dry white bread and one of equally dry Canadian cheese, because, although in full charge now, our cook could not find the butter.

After our meal, the train began to move again, but this time the pleasure was even more short-lived. After only two minutes, the same car jumped the tracks again and got stuck in the soft clay in such a way that, after an hour's work, we decided to call for help by resorting to the telephone, connecting a readily available wire with the telephone line. Everything was so businesslike, and everybody knew so well what to do, that I had the sneaking suspicion

The first derailment

something like that had happened before. Without objection, we submitted to the engineer's stoical persuasion to get ready for the night. As a perfect gentleman, he relinquished his own mattress to you, and, after some consideration, I put it up in the dome, because all of the space was already occupied below. Without undressing you wrapped your blankets around yourself. A few minutes later your regular breathing told me that you had already fallen into deep slumber. Blessed sleep of happy Youth!

Now, with a sigh, I wondered where to find a place for myself. In vain! Everywhere there were people lying about, on the four wooden benches and on the floor. In the dark, I climbed as best as I could over and on top of these contorted figures and finally had no choice but to jump off the caboose and trudge through the deep mud along the embankment to our freightcar. The door was locked, but after my loud banging, it was finally pulled back and Stuart's strong arms helped me climb into the car. Here too, everyone (we counted 26 people in the morning) was stretched out on the floor, and with the help of a miserable lantern I looked for a little space for myself. Finally, I pushed a pair of long legs in huge boots aside and gained some space shaped like a semicircle.

For a long time, the swearing, snoring and telling of jokes continued until finally, our cooking assistant intoned a Methodist hymn:

> Jesus loves me.
> I am very much obliged to Jesus.

At this point, I lost my patience and loudly asked people to be quiet. Against expectations I succeeded in silencing the singer and the joke-tellers, but as a consequence the snoring seemed even louder now. In spite of it, being so tired, I must have dozed off, but suddenly, I abruptly awoke, fearing you might have fallen out of the dome. Since one cannot get rid of such nightmares, I had no choice but to get up instantly. I could reach the other door more easily and I dared jump into the dark landing up to my knees in a water hole. With some difficulty, I climbed out of the hole and groped my way along the cars to the caboose where I found you unharmed and sound asleep. Across from you in the dome, there were the aforementioned small boards. I pushed them somewhat apart and stretched out in the airy gap and actually fell asleep. Every half hour I was awakened by the engineer making his rounds with his little lantern. Towards 4 o'clock it turned ice-cold. I was freezing and envied you for your blankets. With the help of a match I noticed that you had rolled against the wall and that the rain which had begun to fall had found its way through the roof and was dripping on you. I let it drip, covered the damp spot with my hat, climbed next to you and found enough room to protect you from rolling down.

At 6 o'clock, the snoring began to stop in stages, because everyone got up. Using the only wash-basin, one pretended to get clean! In the midst of this activity, the train unexpectedly started to move again! At 8 o'clock, to our surprise, breakfast was served, but what kind of breakfast! These were the leftovers of a meal discovered in the auxiliary car that was standing on the siding of the station.

Another misfortune happened there too. The engineer had retrieved a gramophone, and from that moment on there was not a minute without music! That was the main reason for me to confiscate an empty freightcar. However, it was not completely empty after all. We saw about fifty large bags in its rear part that initially made us quite happy, as we had visions of sleeping arrangements softer than the previous night. The contents turned out to be sugar, and I can safely say that sugar bags make the hardest bed I know. You too did not last more than five minutes trying to sleep on them.

From now on, you already could see the range of the Rocky Mountains quite closely, first the gentle foothills, then the summits of the Bighorn Range and, finally, beyond them the snow-covered peaks of the real Rockies.

We ate very frugally and miserably in a Chinese restaurant in Sylvan Lake where we stopped for an hour for this purpose. It would have been better to keep going and be satisfied with some chocolate. In the evening I first brought the engineer's mattress to our car, then I got you, put you in your blankets, lay down myself next to you and, with the crew around us, and, despite all the snoring, we fell asleep as if lying in comfortable beds.

At 1:00 a.m., there was a loud discourse. We stopped at the station which was the destination for the sugar bags, and three men climbed over us to unload them. I strongly supported Stuart's protest. The three men were kicked out, and everyone went back to sleep except me. I was glad when at dawn we could get up for breakfast which consisted of a piece of dry bread and a sip of tea that was less than per-fect. We could hardly believe it when at 10:00 a.m. we reached the end of the line, Rocky Mountain

House. It had taken two days and two nights for 65 kilometres, and eight times the cars had jumped the tracks. Nobody who reads this short account of a long trip will be surprised to hear that from the log cabin that served as the railway office, I sent several furious telegrams to Toronto.

Then we walked between the two rows of primitive wooden buildings along the wide street to the general store. There we had been offered a real bed for the night, but what a bed! However, the prospect of finally changing our clothes seemed very tempting.

I met the geologist Dowling who had just returned from our mine. The afternoon passed with technical discussions while you played with the dogs and became acquainted with several people. In a French-Canadian restaurant we had a meal that was not too bad and then we went to bed quite happily.

Main Street in Rocky Mountain House

Marcelle waiting again

"Holding Court" in Rocky Mountain House

ROCKY MOUNTAIN HOUSE

ECHO

W. J. KIRBY,
Notary Public, Conveyancing,
Fire Insurance, etc.

C. H. TURNBULL,
Jeweller & Optcian. Issuer of
marriage licenses'.

ROCKY MOUNTAIN HOUSE, ALBERTA,TUESDAY, SEPTEMBER, 17th, 1912

Vol.3.No.17   Whole No51

A party of the Brazeau Coll ieries Company passed through here on September 10th. They were Martin Nordegg, mgr.Dir. of the company, R.W.Coulthard formerly Gen.mgr.of the West Canadian Collieries, now mgr. for this company, his headquarters will be Calgary until next spring; Mr. Gheur, who is the Consulting Engineer and resid ing in Toronto, Mr. Gheur, is a native of Brussels, Belgium: Thos.R.Caldwell, whose father was formerly M.P. for Lanark, he himself being a native of that great county, Stuart Kidd, travelling agent for the company had charge of the party. Mr. Nor degg's daughter was also one of the party, she is going west with her father to christen the new town of Nordegg which will be the first coal mining town west of Rky Mtn House on the Can. Nor. Wes. Ry. Miss Nordegg, is a young lady of 14 yrs and was enjoying the trip immensely.

The town of Nordegg is 110 miles west of Red Deer via rail, the railway follows the Saskat chewan River from Rocky Mtn House to where the Shunda Cr eek empties into it,it then skirts the east bank of Shunda Creek until it comes to The Gap, it then swings over the creek to the south bank and two miles from the gap it will tap the town of Nordegg, which will be a great mining town in another year,as the Company already have a number of men at work there making preparations for putting in a million dollar plant.

Our representive had a long interview with Mr.Nordegg who is a very pleasant gentleman to talk with. He informed us that he expected the Can. Nor. Wes. Ry. would reach Nordegg next May or June, the out put of their mine will then be 2,750 tons per day, Can.Nor.Ry. having contra

cted for the bulk of it, he does not think they will build into the Big Horn or Brazeau Mine for a year or two, the Big Horn being 18 miles west of Nordegg and the Brazeau 37 miles north west and it will cost over $50,000 per mile to extend the line on to those mines and he is con fident that the Nordegg Mine will be quite able to supply the demands until such time as they can extend their line and equip the Big Horn and Brazeau.

The cost of building their Can adian Northern Western Rail way from the C & E line to the town and Nordegg Mine will be $3,800,000 exclusive of the cost of the bridge over the Saskatch ewan River at Rky Mtn House, which will cost $280,000. they will be sending 110 cars of coal a day over this line next year. Rocky Mtn House will be the most important divisional point on this line and Mr. Nordegg is

much pleased with the prospect of this town, as it is such a de lightful situation on the bank of the rivers, he was more than pleased with the rapid strides this town made since his trip here last March, and the termin ius of the C.P.R. line and the yards of the C. N. W. together with the other lines coming in assure Rky Mtn House of being a railroad centre.

It is 56 miles from here to Nor degg, and Mr.Nordegg claims the senery between these two points as most beautiful.At Nor degg just across the creek from the town Mount Colisum raises up in all its grandeur with its snow capped peaks presenting one of the most magnificent pictures that is to be seen any where in the outer ranges of the Rockies.

Mr. and Miss Nordegg and par ty, will go overland from Nor degg to Laggan, passing over the Big Horn Range and the Kootnay Plains, Mr. Nordegg has been over tl at route before and describes it as a delightful ten days trip with mountain senery that is unsurpassed even in Switzerland, and he thinks this will be a favorite route for tourists in the next year or so.

When Mr. and Miss Nordegg arrive at Laggan, they will re turn to their home in Toronto for ten days, the family will then take a trip to Europe; Miss Nordegg will remain abroad for three years attending school in England, France and Germany.

*Shunda Creek is the new name for the stream that has been known as Mire Creek. Shun di being the old Indian name of this stream, shunda is the Cree word for mire.

II

The next morning, we got up early and again began the day with waiting for a very long time. First, your new acquaintances appeared: the engineers of the railway, the manager of the bank, the North West Mounted Policeman and part of our crew. We were sitting on the steps of the general store and held court! Then a team of oxen passed by, driven by the mother-in-law of the editor of the *Rocky Mountain Echo.* Finally, the latter appeared himself and below, you can see what he later wrote about us.

We went down to the Saskatchewan River, climbed a very steep hill to get a view of the construction of the big railroad bridge, then climbed down into a ravine and, for lack of a bridge, crossed a little mountain stream on a tree trunk.

The packtrain, consisting of eighteen horses that had been put together with a great effort, arrived at noon after a long wait. In the meantime, two cowboys, the Belgian engineer, our agent Stuart Kidd, our jack-of-all-trades Tom, you and I took the primitive ferry across the Saskatchewan and awaited the transport that moved with less than haste or hurry. The horses were brought in two sections. As soon as the first one had landed, one of the horses tore loose, jumped into the river and began to swim back despite our shouting and screaming. The current was very strong, and we feared the heavily packed animal might be lost. It fought bravely against the current and was first driven downstream. The horse managed to reach the other shore and was, after some heavy lashing and swearing, placed into the second group of horses that now climbed onto the ferry and landed without further incident.

Crossing a creek near Rocky Mountain House

At last, crew and horses were put together on the other side of the river. You got acquainted with your horse named "Tibby" which from then on would carry you day after day for many hours. It was already decked out with the beautiful leather equipment that my old cowboy Tom Lusk from Texas had braided and cut for you in many a lonely winter hour in Morley whenever he happened to be sober. Everyone admired it while I fastened your raincoat at the back of the Mexican saddle. Then you split your skirt into a divided skirt and mounted your horse in man's fashion. The stirrups were fitted to your boots, and, in youthful enthusiasm, you at once began to trot off with the entire packtrain in pursuit! I caught up with you quickly and punished you by putting you at the end of the packtrain.

Marcelle with Tibby

Preparing the packtrain

We moved at a snail's pace so that the horses could get used to each other and to their rank in the packtrain. After a few kilometres, we reached [the original] Rocky Mountain House, the remnants of the once biggest fort of the Hudson's Bay Company. Only the brick chimneys are still standing. Log cabins and palisades have long since vanished. I told you that more than one hundred years ago, the fort had originally been built by a Scotsman for a rival company, but later it became the property of the Hudson's Bay Company. It was the most westerly fort, was heavily fortified and at times, it housed up to fifty of those brave traders who were at the same time hunters, explorers and inventors, and who had to endure bloody battles with the various Indian tribes.

Marcelle at the head of the packtrain

One of the factors, instead of getting drunk every evening, kept a detailed diary that is well preserved in the Provincial Library in Toronto and presents the most interesting historical document of the Northwest. Not only does the factor report the daily occurrences of trading, he also keeps exact accounts of income and expenses, reports about buffalo hunts, frequent large hunting expeditions and exploration trips by sleigh into the mountains, he lists the names of the white voyageurs, he describes the Indians and their customs, their habits bad and good, and finally gives vivid accounts of their bloody battles. He also refers to climate, topography and stands of trees, and all references definitely appear correct. For instance, he mentions that one had to get the plaster for chinking the gaps of the houses from a spot 3 kilometres to the west near a big tree where an Indian had been hanged for theft. On my frequent rides, I searched for this tree in vain. It probably had been destroyed by lightning, but I finally found the lime deposit.

Chimneys of old Fort Rocky Mountain House

We proceeded along the Saskatchewan River towards the West through open deciduous forest, uphill, downhill, accompanied by the crew singing in minor key the song that we would hear so often from now on:

Oh my Darling ....

After countless repeats without any pause, it was replaced by a merrier one in major key:

> Merrily we roll along, roll along, roll along
> Merrily we roll along over the deep blue swamp

The song was probably adopted from a sailors' song, as you only have to replace "sea" with "swamp," because nobody could have had the idea — not even in jest — to sing about the swamps.

An entire series of acclaimed swear words has been established for generations by the men in charge of packhorses. For me, it meant supreme pleasure to notice how — for your sake — swear words were avoided because to swear in the presence of a lady, no matter how young she may be, is an offense against good manners. And you had to acknowledge that everyone, from the Indians to even the miners, behaved better than "gentlemen of civilization," or, at least some of them did. What I merely have to reproach our people for is their admiring you like a higher being and forever being ready to execute the smallest of your wishes like an order. They even favoured your horse who was patted while the others were lashed.

Just before sunset, we reached a clearing where we made camp for the first time. The packhorses were freed of their heavy loads, then the riding horses were unsaddled, saddles and leather harnesses were collected, the blankets aired. The pack horses were rolling about in the grass to restore their circulation, and the other horses already began to graze. We were all moving around quite lively. Some unloaded the tents, others gathered wood, and the cook unpacked his kitchen utensils and lit a fire. In the meantime, two people looked for poles for the big teepee, better known under the name of "wigwam" which is not used here. In the wilderness, it is the custom never to break or burn these poles but to leave them for others who follow. Not only white people observe this rule, but also the Indians with whom this custom probably originated out of consideration or laziness? Chi lo sa! Thus, one finds these poles everywhere along the trails, usually in such areas where people are hunting, but most certainly near running water. Three of these poles are bound together at their upper ends, while the lower ends are placed on the ground far apart from each other; the canvas cloth is then fastened to a fourth pole that leans against the other three poles, more poles are placed in the gaps between them and the canvas is draped all around them. On one side, there is a chest-high opening, which can be closed by a curtain; this is the only entrance which one can use crawling on all fours. Within a short time you get used to it. One arm pushes the curtain aside, you crawl inside and the curtain is closed again. At the top, the teepee is always open, and at the side there is a movable pole that is turned according to the direction of the wind, to let the smoke from the open fire inside escape effectively.

Whether it rains or snows, there is no cozier place than the teepee with its glowing fire. However, as soon as you get up from your lying position, the smoke stings your eyes so strongly that you have to escape quickly; even mosquitoes and black flies cannot stand it.

With great interest, you had followed the erection of the teepee, and now you watched the pitching of the tent that should serve as a house for you and me. A rope was strung between two trees after being pulled through two holes in the tent. Thus, the tent was hanging already and after driving the pegs into the ground and tying together various ropes, it too was up and ready. After a few days of practice, we could do the entire job in four minutes. I fetched those bags that contained our blankets and I could not help being angry when I noticed among all the bags, it was our bag that had been carried by the horse that had swum across the Saskatchewan River. Since my pack had been packed the wrong way, my blankets had become wet. Fortunately, at least yours had stayed dry. But now I really gave the cowboys hell, which, of course, did not dry the blankets any faster. I spread them in front of the kitchen and the campfires, and, while they were drying, I cut branches from spruce and pine trees, spread them like roof shingles on the floor of our tent, making an elastic mattress, and then demonstrated to you how your bed is made up.

The first camp

First, a waterproof sheet is put on top of the boughs to keep out the moisture from the ground. Next, a woolen blanket is folded lengthwise in three layers which serves as a second mattress in moderate temperatures (in cold weather, however, it provides an additional cover). The second blanket is folded the same way and the open side is secured with safety pins, as is the lower end after having been folded under, so that one's feet cannot stick out. Finally, I put down the pillow that everyone kept smiling about, and which, at bedtime, you even made higher by using your coat. Now your bed was prepared. Next, I prepared my bed, then cut a stick, sharpened one end, smoothed the other end lengthwise, fastened a candle to it, pushed the sharp end into the ground, and our lamp was ready.

By now, it was dark. There is no dusk in this part of the country. We strolled over to the kitchen fire that burned cheerfully. Bacon and beans had been fried in the pan, and now tea was being prepared. A dirty hand grabbed as much as it could from the tea bag, threw the tea into the boiling kettle and then the mistake happened that I could not correct in five years of trying challenges at Canadian campfires: the tea was now boiled for five minutes. The result was an extract of tannic acid the thought of which makes my hair stand on end to this day. For this reason, I mostly drank cocoa that I prepared myself.

The hungry stomachs were now filled, and while we gathered in the teepee to smoke our pipes and chat, you dried the plates, knives and forks that the cook had washed in hot water. Afterwards, you joined us in the teepee and listened to our conversation until we said goodnight and you and I, hand in hand, headed for our tent, stumbling in the darkness over this or that obstacle along the way. I taught you how to undress lying down, because there are no chairs in the tent, and how to fold your clothes in a way that they can be reached at once but stay put in their place. Then I wrapped you in your blankets and, accompanied by the roar of the powerful river, you fell asleep in the light tent for the first time.

At Chambers Creek

As always, I lay awake for many hours, watched the stars glittering through the roof of our tent and listened to the neighing and stomping of the horses that, only bound by their feet, were searching for grass, their only fodder during the entire trip. Those horses, which one suspected of wandering farther away in spite of being hobbled, get a cowbell around their neck, and their melodious ringing could be heard from far away. They were caught at 6 in the morning, and after washing ourselves in the river, we had breakfast consisting of coffee, bread, beans and bacon. Then we broke camp, the horses were packed and saddled, and at 9 o'clock the packtrain was finally on the move again.

It turned out to be a very hot day, and everyone was surprised how well you managed the great hardships. Against all predictions, that you would be tired and stiff after your first days on horseback, you were always livelier in the evening than the rest of us.

When we arrived at the hospital of Camp 4 around noon you, the engineer and I stayed behind and we were invited by the doctor to a welcome lunch. We were hot and hungry and devoured things that we would not have touched in civilized places. The meal progressed very slowly, however, and we constantly had to chase hordes of flies from our plates. The young doctor was very happy about our unexpected visit and would have loved to keep us there for company. After a short rest, we left again and galloped away until we caught up with the packtrain.

Then we continued, always along the Saskatchewan River on its high, steep embankment. I showed you where I had broken through the ice of the frozen river several times last winter while riding in a sleigh. This evening we again made camp close to the river, and both of us slept very poorly. For the first time, you heard the howling of the coyotes (prairie wolves).

The next day, we had to endure a very long and hard ride which kept us in the saddle for ten hours.

Two of this day's events are worth mentioning. Our Belgian engineer who had started riding only a few weeks ago, saw in each horse a roaring, wild animal. In consideration of his lack of experience, he had been given the tamest and oldest animal that did well in the beginning but later in the forest stumbled over every root. Every time he was startled and, instead of helping the horse, he frightened it even more, which may not have been easy for the horse considering its age. Once, unexpectedly falling to its knees, it propelled its rider over its head onto the soft ground, without hurting him in the least, of course. The result: he preferred to march for the rest of the day. We certainly made fun of him, and you, in particular, kept teasing him about the incident.

In the evening, I conducted a little private lecture for him about our mountain horses that are a cross between Indian horses and Hackneys supposedly imported from England. On the back of these animals, which, by the way, are unshod, one feels safer than on one's own feet — be it while climbing uphill or downhill, or crossing roaring rivers, swamps or clearings. But a real friendship between the engineer and any one of the horses, all of which were offered to him one after the other, never developed.

Among the newly purchased horses there was one that never had been ridden before. First, the assistant cook tried to mount it but fell down before he was on top of the horse. Then the cowboy tried his luck, but before we could look again, one of the miners had mounted the horse. Three times it reared without being able to throw him off, and from that time on it was as gentle as a lamb.

By that time, the horses had found their positions in the packtrain and took these now routinely on their own. A cowboy at the head was followed by five packhorses. Stuart, Tom and the second cowboy were followed by five other packhorses. Finally, the two of us with the rest of the crew brought up the rear. Things remained like that until we disbanded the packtrain at the mine. We spent the night on a beautiful, wide prairie in grass as tall as a man that the horses enjoyed, so much so that they did not wander off, and we had no trouble rounding them up the next morning. This camp meant farewell to the Saskatchewan River for more than a week, because the river now turns south in a big bend.

In the teepee that night, we had a long get-together which turned out very interesting. First, Tom started with a funny story about an expedition which he and I had been on together in Eastern Canada years ago. On a very hot day, our engineer Campbell led us from the end of a lake up onto a high hill. Sweating and breathless, we had almost reached the top when Campbell started to scream. He raced downhill shouting "sauve qui peut!" Everyone chased after him, myself in big leaps right behind him without knowing what had happened, until we reached the shore and saw Campbell standing in the water up to his neck and constantly dipping his head into the water. In those days, I was a greenhorn and running downhill I could think of no other reason than that the Indians were after us! Amidst much laughter, I learned that Campbell had stirred up a hornets' nest and had been stung. I, however, had to bear the brunt of everyone's fits of laughter.

Next, we heard an even funnier story about the dignified professor who took part in one of our expeditions — it was his first. He did not find his folded clothes high enough as a pillow; therefore, each night he confiscated a nice, smooth box from our baggage for this purpose. When we had reached our destination, one crew member searched for the box containing dynamite, and when he retrieved it from under the poor professor's head and explained its contents, the latter raced — as he was — into the thickest forest and only after hours of calling, shouting and shooting did we manage to locate him sitting in utter despair under a tree. These stories encouraged everyone to contribute to the conversation and the evening passed merrily with fact and, perhaps, fiction as well.

The next day was very strenuous again. We reached the first mountains and you experienced your first mountain swamp. Your horse Tibby now proved its special skills as a swamp horse by looking for the highest spots and dancing across the swampy spots. At four in the afternoon, we reached Shunda Creek, which we forded six times before reaching our camp. Quickly, you got out your fishing gear and went to the river bank to try your luck. The Belgian engineer, said to be a proven fisherman, took your fishing rod and tried his luck, but in vain. I joined you and said in jest, he did not understand fishing in Western Canada; one had to do it differently. I threw the line high up into some rapids and, to my great surprise, a big brook trout took the bait at once. You clapped your hands in joy and the engineer was no less puzzled than I was. This trout remained the only fish caught — in spite of hours of fishing in which I did not take part any more, just in case.

You had done very well, because on this day, for the first time you had crossed on horseback a roaring mountain stream that reached up to the saddle of your horse. Gradually, by following my example, you learned to cross without getting the soles of your boots wet by pulling your feet up to the horse's neck and crossing the river squatting on the saddle and holding on to the mane. Above all, you had no fear whatsoever, which pleased me the most. For this reason, cowboys and crew had immense respect for you, whose endurance had already surprised them.

At the beginning of our trip, I had had doubts whether a father should expose his still young child to such hardships and dangers, but from this day on, I was reassured. You were the first white female who had ever gone West any further than Camp Shunda. Around the campfire, you laughed about the gloomy predictions for the next day, and even though I knew that the worst of the trip was yet to come, I was not the one to spoil your happy mood.

This evening, a debate about the national economy took place in the teepee. I had claimed that in Canada, a foreigner comes across three names everywhere: first, the Canadian Pacific Railway, the largest organization in the world; second, the firm Massey-Harris, the most important manufacturer of agricultural machinery in the world, whose branch is the first building erected at every new railroad station and sometimes remains the only building there (Massey-Harris sends its machinery to all parts of the world and has even conquered Europe and Germany); and third, the firm Mackenzie & Mann, the owners of the Canadian Northern Railway (Mackenzie had been a village school teacher as recently as twenty-two years ago and Mann a blacksmith; both of these men will soon be the rulers of a railway system reaching from the Atlantic to the Pacific Ocean). These are names that have made Canada great.

The discussion that followed might not have interested you as much as the jokes that ended the evening. The one about the grizzly bear that almost attacked us in our camp two years ago, when we had a young Englishman along whose cartridges we had swiped, because we considered them too dangerous in his hands. Then the story about the fabulous creature which only a few chosen ones get to see and which lives on the mountain slopes and uses two of its legs on the uphill slope so much that they are shorter than the other two. Then the story about the wolf that had opened a stolen can with his snout and could not get it out again. To your credit I have to say, one could not fool you. Finally, we went to bed.

Up to now, I had not spoken on purpose about your Mama [Marcelle's mother], waiting until you would reveal your longing for her. Every night you prayed for her health but now, the first bouts of homesickness hit you and you longed for immediate news which we would not receive for quite some time. After all, until we returned to a railroad station, we would have no contact with the outside world. This is the worst during such trips, and the fearful imagination that something might have happened to one's loved ones is torture, especially during the nights. I consoled and encouraged you that your beloved mother, who lived in far-away Europe, was very well and was thinking of us as constantly as we were of her, and you calmed down and fell asleep.

My thoughts, however, did not let me rest for a long time and that was a blessing. First, there was a rustling noise, then a sudden, unusual brightness and finally a burst of flames. I jumped up and sounded the alarm. Our cooks had not doused the campfire carefully enough; already it had spread and it cost a lot of effort to extinguish it. It could have turned into a real forest fire, and one cannot imagine what might have happened as a consequence. As always, you slept through everything.

The next day, I planned to cover the whole distance to the town of Nordegg, which normally takes one-and-a-half days. We rose at dawn and I rode ahead only with you, a cowboy and the two engineers. We had to pass miles of swamps; as soon as we left one behind us, we were facing the next one. The worst came in a forest of spruce trees where fallen timber barricaded our path across a bottomless swamp. The horses gingerly put their front feet near the roots of the trees and quickly pulled up their hind legs, pushing their bodies close against the trees so that one's right or left leg was in turn pressed against the tree and one screamed with pain. Big holes were torn into one's pants and a few shreds of skin were lost as well. I had already dismounted and the others did the same. But you stayed put and came through without the slightest scratch. We all were puzzled how you managed to do this.

This time, a cowboy led the packtrain, you were next and then me. The engineers brought up the rear. This way I never lost sight of you. When we eventually stopped for lunch, we were very hot and tired. Dry bread, sardines and a drink of water from the cold Shunda tasted wonderful. In front of our eyes, the valley of the river stretched towards the tall mountains whose steep slopes provide a passage for the river. The backdrop was provided by the panorama of the Bighorn Range which had been covered with fresh snow since yesterday.

Shunda Creek

After a short rest, we followed the old trail of the trappers of the Hudson's Bay Company, and you observed that technically, the trail was perfectly laid out with the least possible ascent in mind, so that the railroad engineers could do nothing better than have their line follow exactly the hundred-year-old trail. We had ridden around the shoulder of the mountain to the north and now looked at the mountains of coal formation ahead of us. We crossed the river which in that area is surrounded by swamps on both sides, and ascended the hills to the south. The first sign of the civilization that I had transplanted there was the experimental garden which I had created at an altitude of 4,000 feet, where potatoes, carrots and lettuce have to endure a hard struggle fighting the night frosts. A few minutes later, a dog's barking welcomed us, and, riding through a dense grove of spruce trees, we suddenly spotted the first house in the town that bears your name. Did your heart beat like mine?

Residents of Nordegg

We quickly jumped off the horses, pleased to have completed the first leg of our journey happily and without any accident. The miners had just returned from work and surrounded us while the head engineer welcomed us and gave his report. While the horses were unsaddled, you and I looked at the proud building that serves as office and house for the officials and has a huge set of antlers mounted on the crest of its roof, while the hides of a family of bears, shot a few days ago, were drying at the rear wall. Then we entered the office where we discovered a table, three home-made chairs, two beds and an iron stove.

The first house built in Nordegg

Later, we inspected the town which until that time had only been inhabited by men. You made friends with the cook called "Happy Jack." This was a clever move: he secretly slipped you delicacies such as prunes, raisins, etc. You see, I noticed many things that I did not talk about! After supper, the packtrain arrived which had found the swamps very difficult.

The next few days passed very quickly with lots of work for me and long strenuous hikes around the property, while you entertained yourself with the cook's dogs and puppies and with old magazines.

Then, as arranged, two Stoney Indians visited with whom I discussed the continuation of our trip. They told me that their whole tribe was camped a little more than a day's trip on the other side of the Saskatchewan River across from the mouth of the Bighorn River. After having discussed arrangements for our arrival there, I sent them back well fed and presented with gifts. The next day, you and I went to the mouth of the big tunnel and I showed you our first coal car, built right there.

The first coal mine in Nordegg

Finally, the day and hour of our departure arrived. From here on, our expedition would consist only of Stuart, Tom, you and me besides four pack-horses, until we would reach the camp of the Indians. We said fond farewells to our former travelling companions and, from the door of the big teepee, the Belgian engineer watched us for a long time until we disappeared behind the southern hill. He had not been sad, but rather cheerful, and you could not help making a mischievous remark to Tom that he was glad not to have to come along on the long ride ahead of us.

Marcelle passing time

Stoney Indians

Farewell to the Belgian Engineer

Following the River

III

From the top of the hill we had a gorgeous view of the two mountains to the north: Mount Nordegg* lying to the west, Mt. Coliseum in the east. Then we headed for the Saskatchewan River through dense spruce and deciduous forest. On our narrow trail, we discovered the tracks of a big elk which Stuart declared to be very fresh. We tied the horses to a tree and Stuart alone followed the tracks since you did not want me to leave you. After about 2 kilometres, Stuart took a shot which we did not hear, although we kept very quiet. The meat of this, by the way, "rather old gentleman" served the people of the town of Nordegg for quite a while. They had received the message from Tom whom I had sent back to the town right away. The favour was returned by giving us a dozen very tasty prairie chickens, which we would not have needed. From here on right up to the snowline, we saw prairie chickens very often.

The trail became very difficult now, at times disappearing altogether, and it required a lot of effort to find it again. Finally, it turned into a little-used Indian hunting trail which one could only guess at, and while searching for it, Tom and I lost the two of you. Since you did not respond to our calls, our shouting and whistling any more, and since we did not want to scare you with our emergency signal — a shot three times — we found it to be safest to climb

---

* Officially named Mt. Baldy.

down to the Saskatchewan River. We came upon layers of clay into which we and the horses sank in deeply, and could only get out with great difficulties. In the end, however, we saw you and Stuart on a hill at a distance of about 3 kilometres, your contours sharply set against the sky. Mustering all our strength, we quickly climbed the hill pulling the obstinate horses behind us to within earshot of you. So we were happily reunited, and you had already feared for your almost lost father!

United again, we moved along peacefully through the gravel of the steep embankment of the river. During the numerous descents, we could see far upstream where the river has carved its wide bed through the mountains in countless turns. I secretly succeeded in taking a picture of you crossing one of the many tributaries.

The sun had begun to advance perilously close to the mountain tops of the Rockies when we at last reached the mouth of the Bighorn River. Ahead of us lay a little prairie where my old friend Philip was sitting on his horse eagerly expecting us. After a friendly greeting, he joined us and in answer to the question about the likely weather, which promised to be beautiful, he made a classic pronouncement which you later elevated to an often used saying: "Maybe yes, maybe no, maybe I don't know." Afterwards, you were quite surprised when, suddenly, out of the bush his wife appeared on horseback. You first took her for a man.

We set up camp on the other side of the Bighorn River. I used the hour before nightfall to wash our handkerchiefs and socks in the clear river where little fish frolicked, and then I hung them up to dry by the fire. The ironing I did by pulling everything back and forth along the edge of the packing boxes. Then everything was perfect.

Phillip House

The next morning, we forded the Saskatchewan River, a dangerous undertaking even at the low water-level then. Here, too, you showed no fear, although you got quite wet, but the warm sun dried everything quickly. Soon after, we reached the Indian camp and you met all my friends: Hector, Abraham, Silas and his son, their ladies and their children. They gazed at you in wonderment and admiration. You received a bag made of soft elk skin and a necklace that is said to bring good luck and is made of sweet smelling prairie grass. The Indian called Pete who would accompany us to Laggan [now Lake Louise], said farewell to his people and we rode on.

After a while, the chief who did not understand a word of English, joined us. After a lengthy palaver with our polyglot Stuart, we learned that "Oldman" would like to come along and make himself useful, if we could house and feed him. After a talk with Stuart, who always liked to oblige the Indians, because, as he said, they often had been of great service to him when he urgently needed it, I agreed to take him along, and later, Oldman proved to be very useful, even indispensable. We often asked ourselves what would have happened without him. However, I am convinced we would have managed without him in the end, but certainly not so fast. Because with the following trip we broke the record of crossing the Pipestone Pass by a full six hours.

Crossing the North Saskatchewan River

Superstitious like all children of nature, Oldman did not permit to have his picture taken except when he saw a dollar bill or a big wad of chewing tobacco in front of his nose. Since we travelled without a cent — what would we need money for if there is nothing to buy — and the tobacco was jealously guarded and hidden by Stuart and Tom, I could only take Oldman's picture from behind.

Hector

Joshua and family

Now we were six horsemen again and, counting our packhorses, had to round up ten horses every day. As soon as we had climbed over the next mountain, we saw the beautiful chain of the Rockies in front of us. From then on, we went up and down, mostly through burnt forest that became sparser and sparser, past blue-green mountain lakes the bottom of which we could see and in which the sky with its clouds was reflected, past roaring waterfalls that so often refreshed our eyes, then along dried out riverbeds, until a steep slope forced us to climb up and down again.

Silas and son

Towards evening, a heavy storm broke out. It compelled us to camp at a spot that otherwise we would probably have avoided — a canyon where wood, poles and water had to be fetched from far away. We searched for the latter for a long time, although, Oldman, who never had been in this area before, pointed out the direction with his hand, where water would be found. You bravely marched along because it was I who had assumed the task of bringing the big water-filled kettles back to camp. After half an hour, I had to admit shamefacedly that I could not locate any water.

Oldman

I took you back to the camp but did not want to confess that I had not found any water. So I turned back and discovered the water hole with Stuart's help, who also had to look hard to find it. It was not more than five steps from where you and I had sat to rest and where I had admitted to you that I could not find water. No wonder, it needed more than sharp eyes to notice this hole only one metre in diameter and without inflow or outflow above ground. Otherwise, I would have heard it trickle. During the night, twice a storm ripped off one side of our tent, and with supreme effort and shivering in the cold I tied it together again. Then I fell asleep again and once I thought I heard horses stomping and dogs barking in the distance. I was not sure and I was half asleep, so I put this thought out of my mind as impossible.

The next morning I was awakened by loud shouting and swearing. My dream of horses stomping and dogs barking had been real. As their tracks indicated, two riders and one dog had paid us a secret visit and, instead of leaving their calling cards, they had preferred to steal two sides of our bacon and two loaves of bread. Now a big "council of war" ensued, because the situation had really become serious. We were late by one day, had acquired a big eater, Oldman, whom we had not planned for, and now, four full daily rations had been stolen! The council of war, called a powwow, first speculated about the possible thieves. Friend Oldman, the glutton, who must have been starving himself for weeks — otherwise such an appetite would be impossible for such an old gentleman — could not deny the disappearance of the food, even though he showed a decidedly sad face. He put the blame on the dog and was offended when I could not believe that even a St. Bernard would carry away or eat two big sides of bacon and two loaves of bread.

Tom, in a warlike mood, wanted at once to go on the warpath and follow the tracks. I rejected this "Leatherstocking" idea right away, and now, Tom was offended for which, to our greatest chagrin, we had to suffer during the next meal. My main concern was to come to a decision. So far, everybody, with well-played hypocritical indignation, had rejected my often mentioned desire to hunt for mountain sheep and chamois, as we had done before. Now, I strongly proposed this idea as a necessity. Mind you, we were on the government reserve. Guns are even sealed upon entering the reserve, and stiff fines are meted out for poaching, if one is unlucky enough to encounter an official.

But the reserve is large. There are not many officials around, and, as the minister in Ottawa told me earlier, one just must not get caught. Two years ago, we roasted a few juicy legs of mountain sheep over a fire when two police officers appeared. They invited themselves to dinner and complimented us, with a twinkle in their eyes, about the well-preserved sheep legs that we had transported on our packhorses for several hundred miles in the summer heat. Then, my old cowboy, Lusk, was so bold as to hand one of the officials the well-wrapped horns, asking him to send them to the hotel in Calgary where we later received them. The reason for this transaction was that upon leaving the reserve it can happen that at the slightest suspicion, one's baggage is checked and then one gets into serious trouble, if anything illegal is discovered.

So, after the hypocritical resistance, my final word won at last. Or, maybe it was the dreaded hunger — I rather think it was the latter. Besides, I promised to bear all the consequences myself, and I drew their attention to the neighbouring province of British Columbia and its law that "need knows no law," permitting every voyageur to hunt as much food as he requires for his sustenance.

On the high trail

This time, you were very impatient and galloped ahead along the valley. I followed and held my beautiful camera in my hand which during this fast ride hit the saddle-horn just once, but from then on it only worked occasionally despite immediate repairs. You received a severe talking-to and were banished to the end of the train again.

That day turned into a real climbing tour, the men mostly on foot in order not to overtire the panting horses. For the last time, we left the Saskatchewan — when will you ever see it again — crossed the two Divides and quickly reached the high mountains. We set up camp at the Siffleur River, which was swarming with trout.

In the teepee during the nightly chat, we told you about the tribe of the Stoney Indians, direct descendants of the Sioux, about the bloody battles they fought against their cousins, the Bloods and the Prairie Indians, who pushed them back more and more into the mountains. When finally peace prevailed, the long struggles with the white intruders began and, finally, the "Rebellion" which many contemporaries took part in, as for example the father of your friend Dora Wilson in Banff.

We told you how this once powerful tribe was reduced to about one thousand souls, that many became Methodists while their elders still believed in the medicine man and in Manitou, that the children attend school occasionally and that the women are burdened with all the heavy work to this day. The men still go hunting as their main occupation, even though this is now forbidden. The skills acquired over generations not only left them with an incredibly sharp eye and a fine sense of smell, but also gave them a sixth sense, an absolutely reliable sense of orientation and the sense for the presence of drinking water.

But even we white people who often have to depend on our own resources when we venture into the wilderness, develop a sense for the direction towards the North which becomes our second nature, even when neither sun nor stars are of help. If one does not have that sense, it is better not to leave the beaten path or there will surely be trouble. Many people have been lost in the mountains and only a few were found again. If one has this sense, however, one is absolutely sure to find the path again which always proceeds according to definite laws.

When the Indians become civilized, they often lose this sense very quickly, because they concentrate on farming and cattle-raising, where they earn good money. In that case, of course, they do not live as nomads in tents any longer, but build log houses which, however, are as dirty and full of insects as the teepees. In shedding their blanket-coats, the Stoneys demonstrated the abandonment of the traditions of their forefathers, but they never parted with their little braids that fall forward at both sides of their head and are only undone once a year to be greased with bacon.

Stuart told you of the habits and customs of the Indians, weaving a few fairy tales into his stories, and then he talked about the indelible superstition and unbelievable vanity of these children of nature. But even among them there are already some who allowed modern education to successfully affect their lives. One example is our surveyor Tom Green, who is a full-blooded Indian and yet passed the university exams in Montreal with summa cum laude. Another Indian became a successful real estate speculator, mainly, as the saying goes, through the influence of his squaw who has the evil eye of the cross-eyed.

All this probably followed you into your sleep because you constantly tossed from one side to the other. Or was it the hair-raising tea that had been particularly strong? The small dwarf-spruce trees creaked in the wind and bothered one's sleep. Therefore, it was not hard to get up and admire the sunrise in all its splendor. Since I was determined to reach the Pipestone Pass that day, we first had to have another long discussion and then a very long and strenuous ride, the grand scenery of which made us forget all our efforts.

I remembered how four years ago, on the eastern slope of one of the mountains we had sighted a herd of mountain sheep and had shot two of them. I mentioned this to our Indian whose face showed disbelief because the described altitude seemed too low to him. As a cautious diplomat, he did not say much, only moved his upper body as usual from one side to the other. His feet, clad in soft pearl-embroidered moccasins, accompanied this swaying by beating a regular tact on the flanks of the horses. In addition to his leather jacket and the soft leather pants which, by the way, were the only clothes he was wearing, to-day he had taken from his saddle-bag the woolen coat with the many colourful stripes and the hood, and had wrapped it around himself, because despite the beautiful sun, it had turned quite cold.

The never-ending silence of the Canadian solitude is oppressive to the newcomer. Even in the forests there are no songbirds, very rarely a squirrel in the evergreens which will flee into the treetops angry about any disturbance. In the burnt-out forests and in the high mountains, there is moaning and groaning when in the wind one half-fallen tree trunk rubs against another. Apart from that, particularly in the high mountains, there is no sound disrupting the silence. Not even the horses neigh. They gingerly put foot after foot on the ground which they first test with their eyes and nostrils. And so it goes for hours: a solemn, almost gloomy silence that leaves no one unaffected. The merry songs we enjoyed on the plains during our first days had long since ceased; so this grand scenery would affect us without disturbance or diversion.

But it is at night, that noises awake! First, the trees of the forest play entire scales in the wind. Then the animals, especially the wolves. Often, we heard the muffled growling of bears that lurked close to the camp, and sometimes the shrieking of elks, the grunting of stags and the strange calling of cows. Occasionally one heard the hissing and screaming of lynx and the whistling of marmots.

The horses sometimes called each other with their neighing, and we soon learned to recognize yours by its lighter sound. From the first day on, you had gotten used to your horse, but you were disappointed when it did not want to take a piece of sugar as a reward. It was still an unspoiled child of nature that did not know the charms of luxury. You rewarded it by patting and stroking and made friends with him, and with confidence about your absolute safety in the saddle, you followed my example and absorbed the beauty of the mountains, the clouds and the blue sky. You looked left and right, far into the distance, and you learned to look out for yourself, to look around and to ask. And when you began to get tired in the saddle, you changed your position, turning one leg over to the other like a lady in a sidesaddle, which I also often did, and this way, you could even look backwards.

Since I had awakened your interest in botany, we never rode past the smallest flower to which you would not draw my attention and often, I quickly jumped off the horse to pick one of the flowers for you. Do you remember when I showed you where the upper line of growth of vegetation was? It was there that I picked a few flowers and pressed them in my notebook for you.

The high Rockies

We climbed over another mountain and descended into a long valley. Both of its sides were bordered by high mountain ridges, their crests covered in eternal snow. Now, the vegetation consisted only of grass and heather. Through the valley, the narrow Siffleur River wound its way, and in the soft sand still smooth from the last thaw and the last flood, I showed you the old tracks of lynx and wolves, also a few newer ones of a little grizzly bear and, finally, very fresh ones of a herd of mountain sheep.

Your justified question whether animals would not sometimes attack people I could answer in a re-assuring way, because on my many long rides I always observed that animals avoid people. Only their curiosity often makes them stay around people and have a look at these strange creatures — their deadly enemies. Repeatedly, I saw elk emerging from the forest, saw them watch us, disappear, re-appear, look again, but flee at the slightest noise. You understood that I did not have the heart any longer to destroy this trust with a bullet but preferred to take pictures instead.

One very rarely hears witnessed accounts of animal attacks. The females of the animals probably attack when they sense danger for their young ones, and if this happens to be a grizzly, the result is always a tragedy. Because one bullet, even one with a soft coat, will never kill the bear with one shot through its heart. And for a second and third shot there is usually no time, except when you are not unprepared but rather on a regular hunt with your rifle ready to shoot. When animals are wounded they also attack, like the elk in the East two years ago which trampled to death an official of the Canadian Geological Survey whose rifle failed at the second shot.

The cold wind hitting our faces interrupted our chat and we climbed higher and higher in the valley that now wound its way high up. The sun disappeared behind the clouds, and a light shower sprinkled down on us; it already was mixed with snow flakes. Suddenly, I saw how our old Indian who was always twenty metres ahead of the train, stopped and pointed with his hand to a mountain range. In spite of my excellent "Trieder" binoculars I could see absolutely nothing and so I galloped as fast as I could past the packtrain to its head. Stuart, who could not spot anything either, followed. He interpreted for me that the Indian was seeing a herd of about eight mountain sheep grazing up on a mountain slope. We continued riding quietly and slowly until we reached the same altitude and then stopped in a small open forest.

After dismounting and seeing the sheep, by quietly using our binoculars, the atavistic urge to hunt got hold of me again, and I asked Stuart for the rifle as I wanted to climb up with the Indian Pete. You, however, would not let me go in spite of my assurance that nothing could happen to me, because nothing had ever happened to me in the past. You were so worried about me that I gave in to you. With a heavy heart, I let Stuart go with the Indian and followed them with my eyes for a long time. Now we could quite clearly distinguish the herd. It moved slowly along the side of the mountain. A few hundred metres above them, the old Indian pointed out to me, were three mountain goats.

We now hurried to unsaddle the horses, unload the packhorses, and pitch the tents before dark. But in the middle of this hard work which Oldman, Tom and I had to carry out alone this time, a snowstorm broke out which within a few minutes blew everything upside down and covered it with snow. My first thought was to roll up the blankets and wrap my coat around them. But then, I tore down the half-pitched tent and spread it on the ground to secure a small dry spot for us, then ran over to Tom and helped him and the Indian to pitch the teepee. While Tom and I carried the packs to safety, the chief had already fetched water and cut wood so that you could quickly get warm and be protected in the teepee and could dry your things.

We continued to work outside in the snow. First, Oldman and I pitched our tent, spread the blankets, prepared everything for the night, and then I could finally stomp over to you in the teepee and get dry myself. In the meantime, you had helped Tom with the kitchen, and we just debated whether we should eat alone or wait for our hunters when we heard shots far in the distance during a break in the howling, whistling storm. We decided to wait for them. We chatted for two hours and it was almost 9:00 p.m. when a jolly hello announced the arrival of the two, the curtain was pulled open, first a dead little white mountain goat appeared, then Stuart, then the hind leg of a mountain sheep and finally the Indian.

The two looked like snowmen. They were wet, cold and hungry, and, only after a long while did we get them to talk.

The climbing expedition in the rubble along the steep slope had required moving on all fours, and, when they finally reached the narrow ledge overgrown with grass where further ahead the herd was grazing, both men were so exhausted that they had to stretch out flat on the ground to catch their breath. Then, Stuart crept straight ahead while the Indian crept higher up, because there was only room for one on the ledge. After crawling about 200 metres, Stuart came around a protrusion and saw more than a dozen sheep calmly grazing about 50 metres away. Rifle to cheek and "piff-paff-puff" — these were the three shots we had heard. What followed happened quickly. The Indian who crept above Stuart had also fired but lost his footing and came crashing down towards Stuart. Two sheep had tumbled down; a third, badly wounded, limped after the fleeing flock. Stuart raced towards the falling Indian. He grabbed the rifle to which the Indian still clung, and, with all his strength, Stuart propped himself against the mountainside and stopped the Indian's fall.

As soon as they were back on their feet, they ran after the herd on the now widening path, but, of course, could not see the herd any more, not even the wounded animal.

Instead of returning on the same path they had used before, they climbed to where the Indian had wanted to get in the first place, and, in the falling darkness they spotted four mountain goats. Stuart killed the kid and the Indian the father. Then the snowstorm, which we had already endured for quite a while, caught up with them. On the slope, they rolled the animals down hill, and then climbed down after them, finding their prey at the bottom.

While they were telling their story during the storm, I noticed how you looked at the poor little animal that seemed to stare at you with its glassy eyes and how you turned away in horror. Later, we could not persuade you to try eating the game. We walked to our tent whose one wall had collapsed under the snow. I shook the snow off with great effort and then we tried to sleep.

The next morning turned out to be a very miserable one. Our people did not want to move on, not only because they were tired, but also because the horses were so wet with snow that they could not be packed. The real reason, however, was quite a different one. The Indians are used to staying put after a hunt until everything is eaten. So, why transport the game? Once his teepee is set up and water and meat are available, any place looks beautiful for the Indian, and there is no reason to exchange it with another one.

I therefore had to work hard to get my way this time. I told them one could not remain up here anyway, and that there was no other way out but to cross the big pass as fast as possible. And we should not rule out the possibility that a police patrol might come by which would get us all into trouble. After endless palavers, the sun helped me conquer the tough resistance. Before we quickly packed up, I photographed the teepee, that we had set up so miserably, being in such a big hurry during the snowstorm the previous evening.

I knew what lay ahead for us on this day, and so you had to put on — not without resistance on your part — my heavy woolen vest and all sorts of other warm clothes. How strongly you resisted at first and how cold you got in spite of at last giving in!

It was a bad day for humans and for animals. First, the Indian rode off to hide the biggest portion of the bounty in the forest, although of all the people crossing this pass, only Tom Wilson does so several times each year. When Pete caught up with us he brought along more meat including the head of a mountain goat whose little black horns fascinated you and, now mounted, always remind you of that evening high in the mountains.

Today, our horses crawled as slowly as the minutes passed in this icy wind. The wind penetrated to one's very marrow, sweeping from behind in the direction of the long pass. A thin layer of snow covered the swamp where the Pipestone has its source, and it became very difficult for the horses and ourselves to avoid holes and rocks. We ate lunch in the saddle so as not to hold back the horses that could not find any food up there. Slowly, new mountain ranges moved into view like sets in a theatre, but, straight ahead, the pyramid, that marks the end of the pass, remained in sight and forced us to take a detour to the left. This was proof that the summit of the pass does not coincide with the Divide that we had crossed long before, while up to now we still had to climb higher and higher. But now we had reached the highest point and from here on, the snow had been swept away by the strong wind that had grown into a storm. Ahead of us lay a rocky desert and to the left and right the mountain ranges covered with eternal snow. We shivered in the cold. The icy storm brought tears to our eyes and I noticed how badly you had to suffer.

Before the descent

The rubble became deeper, and, to relieve the poor, panting horses, we again climbed uphill. To avoid exposing ourselves too much to the storm, we dismounted and continued our ascent, leading the horses by the reins. On the ground, I noticed a rock that showed the imprints of plants and I succeeded in distracting you for a short while. I put it into my pocket, and now it sits in front of you, serving as a paperweight. May it remind you, my dear child, that even the most difficult hours pass. And these were really tough hours that you stood very bravely.

The wind almost blew us over the sharp ridge (2,560 metres) and we looked down into the long valley of the Pipestone River. First, an elongated swamp, then a trickle of water, then a creek and, finally, the river that runs into the Bow near Laggan. How many times did we have to ford the Pipestone! Did you count? Twenty-one times! We mounted our horses again which had also become more cheerful and faster once we went downhill. Gradually, the wind calmed down, and, since the valley turned Southwest, we got the last rays of sunshine directly into our faces.

This time, we set up camp at 4:00 p.m., and I was therefore determined to start all the earlier the next day. After all, I had mapped out my programme to be in Laggan the next day and I stubbornly wanted to get my way. The horses found welcome feed in the high grass along the creek. We rested all afternoon, had fresh meat, and were happy to have the pass behind us. Then why not set out on a vigorous march with the prospect of seeing the railroad again at the end of it, and finally a real hotel with four walls and a solid roof, with beds and baths, chairs and tables and clean clothes!

These probably were the thoughts that passed through your little head; they were mine too, but I knew that with me this joy would not last very long. When the snow has melted and the mountain valleys cover themselves with green and the strong wind sweeps from the glaciers, then I hear the call of the "Red God." I am drawn to the mountains and I forget all the upcoming difficult hours, and I cannot rest until I have tasted the first burnt bacon again and have been annoyed about the always bitter tea.

But why spoil the prospect of the beautiful tomorrow with the outlook to the sadder day-after-tomorrow?

Anyway, I was absolutely determined to try our utmost, and not even the usual passive resistance that presented itself again at the following powwow could hold me back. I ordered the departure for 6:00 a.m. which means gathering the horses at 4:00 a.m. Then I followed the useless example of a tree-abuser and cut your name, the names of the crew, the number of horses and the date into a big Douglas fir. At a small creek which runs into the Pipestone further downstream, I had our tent pitched and, for the last time I prepared a soft bed of spruce branches for you.

After we had eaten our supper, the moon was already high up in the sky, although it was only 8 o' clock. You went into the tent to put everything out for the night, and when you did not return to the teepee after half an hour, I walked over to the tent and cautiously peeked inside. While unpacking you had fallen asleep. I covered you with both blankets in order not to wake you. You were sleeping soundly when I went to bed, and when the first rays of the sun woke me and I in turn had to wake the other people, you were still sleeping and even the commotion following, rounding up the horses, breaking camp, cooking, eating breakfast did not disturb you. Finally we took down your tent and carried it away and the sun laughed into your face and so did we! Then you jumped up quickly, got dressed just as quickly. You hastily ate a few bites and off we went!

The lower we descended, the denser the forest became. Sometimes to the right or to the left we were in fallen timber, once we even had to climb a mountain through fallen timber, which was a hard piece of work. Then the path improved and you and I galloped ahead to encourage the crew to ride faster. By 11 o'clock we really felt hungry. We always ate a meagre breakfast, because who can eat bacon and beans early in the morning? Since we were far ahead of the packtrain — the source of our food supply — we had to wait patiently for it.

I chose a small mountain whose steep slope, descending towards the river, offered an unobstructed view. We tied the horses to a tree and flung ourselves down on the soft ground covered with spruce needles. You cradled your head in both hands and looked at the splendid alpine landscape that spread out in front of our eyes like a panorama. Mountain range after mountain range towered towards the West topped by the huge Mt. Sir Donald reaching into the sky in the distance, and masses of snow and glaciers glistened in the sunshine. And below you, the wild mountain stream rolled along whose childhood you had seen only yesterday and which by to-day had grown quite noticeably now roaring down the valley.

We turned around, and, before we even discovered the packtrain, a soft ringing of bells announced its approach. With our horses we went down to the river, forded it together with the train and shortly after stopped for lunch at an idyllic spot. This time, we unpacked the last delicacies which we had saved as a special reward. Often, the thought of them had given us energy but not the courage to attack the tin of sardines in tomatoes, the tin of apricots and the dried pea soup in the shape of a sausage. This time, we did have the courage and we had a big feast. I told the crew that you and I would definitely reach Laggan to-day, and if they would not get that far, they should report to the hotel the next morning. We then said farewell to the two Indians, one of whom, the Chief, wanted to take the train from Laggan to Morley, while our Pete was to ride back at once across the Pipestone Pass to Nordegg.

The rest of us left to cross a large windfall, and then I rode with you alone as fast as the path would permit. When we forded the river for the last time, we already saw signs of civilization: the trees on the other shore had branches cut off, while empty tins and boxes told us of a picnic that courageous visitors from Laggan had held here. Afterwards, we reached a large swamp which then was very wet. Because of the tall grass, I could no longer recognize our trail. With great effort, I found it again on the other side and for a short while we proceeded briskly. Then we encountered a windfall that required so many detours that we lost the tracks again. The trees were piled denser and denser. We had already dismounted and were drenched with perspiration from climbing over the trunks.

Employing my long experience, I anticipated the location of the trail, providing it was cut correctly. I pointed out the spot where it would be accessible to us at the shortest distance. You were not just a little surprised when I really found it there. A load fell off my chest as, because of you, I had become a little worried. The horses had become weak and stumbled over every root, but still, we moved on. The sun was slowly setting, and again we came up against a swamp. This time I hopelessly lost the trail. Now it became clear to me that already at the first swamp we had turned too far east and instead of taking the higher-lying summer trail, we had taken the closer but lower-lying winter trail that leads across the swamps that are frozen in winter.

It was important now to keep one's spirits up and turn west. Uphill, it worked well, but on top we encountered a windfall through which we had to fight our way step by step. Then it began to get dark. I sensed how you began to lose your courage, although you did not say a word. To distract you I told you, while we caught our breath, how awful I had felt once when we also lost our track and had to sleep in the forest without food or tent.

The trunks were now lying very close to each other, your horse stumbled and I asked you to leave it behind, I could always get it fifty steps later. And that is what I did, even though this way I had to take each step twice.

Now the worst happened — a swamp in the middle of the forest where we as well as the horses sank in deeply. After, with luck, we had rescued ourselves from this obstacle, your energy had reached its limits. We rested and I explained to you that we now would turn west, travel in a straight line and find the path shortly. But first we had to get around this terrible swamp. Your courage returned, we turned back, took a wide semi-circle and could not go on! That was when our troubles were at their worst, I admit. At that moment, even I feared that I would have to spend that night with you in the forest.

Windfall

In my mind, I was already cutting branches for fire and thinking the two horse blankets would be sufficient to keep you warm. I quickly reached into my pocket to convince myself of the presence of our last chocolate bar. Suddenly, the howling of a locomotive sounded in the distance. Our courage returned instantly. We jumped as though electrified. I asked you to stay behind while I again went looking for the path. I jumped over the tree-trunks, avoiding the swampy spots, and to my great joy found the summer path that was running along the highest ridge west of the mountain and had not been built entirely according to the rules of the game. I hurried back to you and your horse, then rushed back to get mine.

Now we climbed uphill. What a joy! The poor, exhausted horses started to trot on their own. The path widened, we crossed a rough wooden bridge, and soon after, three abandoned houses appeared where lumberjacks used to live. In the now rapidly growing darkness, we finally saw the lights of the station at Laggan. We raced down the mountain. The horses became covered with perspiration in spite of the cold evening air. They shied at every little piece of paper, every box, at anything unusual along the way. And now we heard the barking of a dog.

Before reaching the station, we had to cross the railway tracks and there the horses refused to obey. With great effort, we succeeded to lead them around a freight train across the tracks, and finally we reached the station. From there, a 5 kilometre long beautiful winding road leads to the Chalet, the hotel of the Canadian Pacific Railway. The lights of the hotel served as our guide, because it had turned pitch dark in the meantime.

Then, we galloped into the yard of the hotel and jumped off our horses, which a boy right away led into the stable. I entered the hotel, was assigned our rooms and received a big package of letters and several telegrams from which — after opening them with a pounding heart — I learned to my great joy that your mother was well. And then, I turned around to give you the good news.

I was puzzled not to find you. I finally discovered you behind a pillar at the entrance of the hotel. You were hiding because you did not want to be seen in your "clothes of the wilderness" by the hotel guests, who were mostly wearing evening dress. I coaxed you and scolded you but nothing helped. You refused to enter the dining room. Since we men like to make concessions to the female gender, I ordered through room service a meal that seemed most delicious to us, and, with a bottle of champagne, we finished our repast, toasting our happy homecoming.

That evening, I had a lot to do with the sending of cables, telegrams, looking through the mail — then at 10 o'clock Tom announced by phone from the station the happy arrival of the packtrain. After the first bath — that was followed by two more every day from then on until we began to feel reasonably clean — we went to bed. But neither of us slept very much. Was it the unaccustomed soft bed, or the heat of the room in spite of the open windows, or was it the lovely feeling to have a solid roof over our heads again, or was it the greater quantity of food, or maybe even the champagne?

IV

As usual, we got up very early. The suitcases arrived which we had shipped from Edmonton by train, and with the clothes of civilization we dared show ourselves to the astonished folk in the hotel. Only now did I notice how tanned you were. While we were on the terrace of the hotel, admiring the grandiose panorama of Lake Louise and the Victoria Glacier, Tom and Stuart appeared, still in their cowboy suits. They hardly recognized you, and when later they adopted the clothes of civilization, you confided in me that they had looked much nicer before.

The next day, we travelled to Banff where I expected to meet the engineers and officials. On the train we again met — strangely enough — the geologist Dowling who travelled east from the Pacific Ocean. He paid you many compliments for your endurance in having accomplished this strenuous, dangerous ride in record time. In Banff, the following days passed very quickly for you. There you had your friend Dora Wilson. We were always a large group there, and you practiced your wit with our friends as they did with you. During the first night it began to snow heavily and did not stop the following days either.

The big hotel, still a wooden structure that finally is being rebuilt to be fireproof, is so comfortable that even in bad weather, one can live there very well. The view is gorgeous. To one side Mount Rundle loomed. In front of it a bridge spanned the Bow River. Along its shores, golf links were now laid out.

Strange, these English people! Wherever they go in the world, they bring along their national customs and keep them for generations: whiskey, golf and tennis — the only nation on earth that never loses its identity and its national self-confidence in its rulers. The Germans who once were embarrassed to be recognized as Germans, have recently displayed greater self-confidence that unfortunately is quite often exaggerated and then becomes very unpleasant. However, it is better this way than the former anxious hiding of their nationality.

Often we went down to the big waterfall where four years ago you caught trout every day, then looked at Sulphur Mountain on the other side of the hotel with the observatory on top. You remembered how at that time we had climbed up and had enjoyed the beautiful view of the mountains to the North from which we had emerged only a few days ago. We then climbed down to the river, drove also to Lake Minnewanka, whose depth could not yet be measured and where yard-long fish are caught.

On our return trip we passed the National Park where red deer, elk and the last buffaloes are kept fenced. We also visited the interesting little museum with its handsome zoological garden that houses the animals of the Rocky Mountains: brown, black and grizzly bears, wolves, lynx, eagles, vultures, but no sheep or goats.

From the hotel's pavilion, which is protected by large window panes, we watched the sunset and after dinner, during which time you young folks joked and laughed a lot, we listened in the great hall to the concert of the small band. We were standing at the banister of the upstairs gallery which runs alongside the great hall, when to my not small surprise I observed a little intermezzo: can you imagine, Stuart stuck out his tongue at you — and you did the same. But Marcelle! For a long time after, this provided us with a reason to laugh, and I hope you were just as embarrassed as the forever child-like thirty-five-year-old Stuart.

Later, we sat in front of the big fireplace where the huge logs are glowing and crackling even in summer. I drew your attention to the inscriptions on the mantelpieces of the two fireplaces. These inscriptions, whose author is said to be Thomas Payne, actually made a long journey from Palestine to the lonely, rocky "nest" in the Rocky Mountains, as they originate from the Talmud:*

> The world is my homeland, travelling is my teacher, to do good is my religion, and people are my friends.

Engraved in stone on the other mantelpiece the next inscription reads:

> God gave us our relatives. Praise to God that we can always choose our own friends.

And, below the big mirror, one reads:

> The world is a mirror. Try always to smile into it.

Take the latter to heart and the world will always beam back at your smiling face.

---

* Martin Nordegg is mistaken. The quotes are actually taken from Hammurabi, King of Babylon around 1950 BC.

Towards noon, when the sun was shining on the white winter landscape, we went down to the open pool area which contains one large basin with hot and one with cold water and watched Stuart, Tom and Perry who tried their swimming tricks there. There was a lot of splashing and laughing until I dragged you away and after a short hike showed you the hot sulphur springs with the beautiful grotto and the stalactites and I told you that these springs had, of course, been known to the Indians for a long time, and they had used them for healing purposes.

At the end of the trail

The general claim that Indians have an aversion to bathing was destroyed for me a long time ago, since I had so often discovered their "Turkish Baths" in the mountains: a large basket made from willow branches covered with furs into which the Indians put hot stones and stand on them to sweat. However, these baths are medicinal means of healing, and I never noticed any other ways of washing with the Indians. You, of course, were luckier, because you saw that Pete once washed his face and dried it with the dish towel. But that must have been Pete's mistake.

While we sat in front of the fireplace, Stuart asked me to tell the story of my first encounter with a mountain sheep that became known only too quickly among all the cowboys in Morley. It happened during my first expedition to the Rockies. After a 14-day ride, starting at Morley, we finally reached the Bighorn River, and, in spite of the pouring rain, I decided to inspect the first coal deposits with our geologist McEvoy. We had sent the tired horses back to camp and I asked McEvoy to hike back with me from the big waterfall. We walked along the high embankment of the canyon — a path that winds like a snake.

We were not far from our camp anymore when I drew McEvoy's attention to a big rock that was lying on a ledge near the opposite shore. McEvoy said that, geologically speaking, the rock was an impossibility. It had to be an elk. We stood there quietly, but since the elk did not move, McEvoy changed his opinion. We continued slowly. Suddenly, I got the feeling the rock had moved. McEvoy did not want to believe me and suggested I should fire a shot in its direction. I had my Mauser pistol ready when I got second thoughts. I might appear totally ridiculous in the eyes of the cowboys and Indians if I shot a rock.

So McEvoy said I should aim the pistol, he would walk on and should I see something move again, I should fire. If he should see anything, he would raise his arm. I looked across, then to McEvoy and just then he raised his arm. With sights set at 200, the first shot burst — the rock did not move. I was ready to set the safety catch and follow McEvoy, when he came running back calling out to me it was a big red elk. I sent over two more bullets and now the rock rose and went slowly into the underbrush.

Since I considered myself a perfect shot, even though in the West I had not yet proven myself, I was very embarrassed, the more so, as McEvoy had guessed the distance at 300 and I had contradicted him. And while we still discussed the matter, the elk reappeared, stood on the ledge and looked in our direction. With sights set for 150, I sent over two more bullets and with a big leap the animal disappeared into the trees. I wanted to return to the waterfall to ford the river, which ran high, at the only possible spot. But McEvoy considered this impossible without horses. So, we went to the camp and I related the event, feeling very embarrassed. I sure was made fun of, even though with its respect for me, the crew did not dare to laugh too openly. I, however, did not want to believe that I had failed. I was sure of my shots, or at least of one of the five. I went over to the tent of the Indians.

Philipp had his squaw and two papooses along, and I talked with him and tried to get him to saddle his horse and ride back to the spot.

He replied, "How much?"

I promised him five dollars, if he would find the animal and bring back its head. At first he seemed to be agreeable, but then he had another question, how much he would get if his search in the pouring rain was unsuccessful. Since I was so sure of this matter myself, I promised him two dollars in this unlikely case. He agreed and I returned to the camp. After three hours, the honest Philipp came into the teepee and said, "Nothing found." I gave him the promised two dollars and was very annoyed.

Eight days later, after our return from Brazeau, we came down the other side of the canyon and I begged McEvoy to ride with me to the never forgotten ledge, supposedly to view the area from there. Not ten meters from the ledge, next to a tall spruce tree lay a huge mountain sheep, half eaten by wolves. That was my animal. McEvoy looked dumbfounded. We had somebody fetch the skull with the big round horns that now decorate my room.

We, however, held "criminal court" over Philip. This fellow had not even left his tent until he thought the time had come to get his two dollars. These we deducted at the next payment of his wages. Since then, he has become a good friend to me. Perhaps he waits for another opportunity to get back his two dollars one way or another. I, however, have become the object of a lot of laughter around many a campfire — it is unbelievable how fast a story like that can spread.

The few days in Banff passed much too fast. We said good-bye to our friends and took the train to the West again. On this trip to the Pacific Ocean, from the comfortable Pullman car, you would again admire the grand scenery of the Rocky Mountains which before you had observed from the saddle while coming from the North. We passed Laggan again, its three lakes in the clouds, then the Great Divide where two little streams originate, one flowing towards the Pacific Ocean as a tributary of the Columbia River, the other towards Hudson Bay as a tributary of the Saskatchewan River.

Then we raced through the narrow, deep canyon of the Kicking Horse River to which the courageous explorer Palliser gave this name after an adventurous incident, then around the base of the powerful, mighty Mt. Stephen at whose slopes one can still see, 762 metres above the train, the tunnel of a long abandoned lead-silver mine, then along the new section of the railroad that leads through the two biggest tunnels in America. And since the American can only admire something if numbers impress him, the following should be mentioned: one-and-a-half million dollars, total length 2 kilometres, 75 loads of dynamite which alone cost a quarter-million dollars. These are the tunnels under Mt. Ogden and Cathedral Mountain whose construction I deplore. Before, descending in large curves one saw the entire beautiful scenery. Now, like a snake the railroad winds its way in spirals through the interior of the mountains and crosses the river only twice.

Now, we approach Field, and to the north we notice the colony "Edelweiss" of the Swiss alpine guides who are brought across the ocean by the railway company every year, although there is not much climbing taking place. The Ottertail group towards the south looks like the "Oetztaler Ferner" [a glacier in Austria] and Mount Goodsir stretches its long fingers into the blue sky. Then we reach the canyon where the train constantly seeks shelter, moving from the right shore to the left and back again, and where the thundering train and the racing river awaken hundred-fold echoes. Finally, there is the station of Golden, then Moberley where I showed you the old wooden hut of the first railroad engineers who spent the severe winter of 1870-71 there.

From now on, it is downhill in the valley of the Columbia with a splendid view of the Selkirk group. The most northern point of the railroad is Beavermouth, then it turns towards the southwest. We leave the Columbia and race along the Beaver River, climb again and reach the summit at Rogers Pass. Before that, however, you admire the beautiful Mount Sir Donald and Mt. Tupper, also Swiss Peak named after the first person to climb it, a member of the Swiss Alpine Club.

Rogers Pass runs between two snow-covered ranges that had never been touched by a human being before the year 1882, as the trading between the Indians from the Coast and those from the Prairie was conducted via the Howse Pass. And now, we reach the Selkirk Summit with its indescribable panorama of snow-covered summits, the likes of which you probably cannot see from a train anywhere in the world. From now on, snowshed follows snowshed to keep the tracks well protected and free of avalanches. These sheds were the first engineering work by Mackenzie and Mann who in those days could not even put up security of $5,000.00 and had to borrow the money from the Grey Nuns in Montreal.

Next comes the station of Glacier with the big Illecillewaet Glacier which one can reach quite comfortably without any effort and into which the Swiss guides cut tunnels. Then, we go down the winding river and finally, we are in Revelstoke. We bid farewell to the "High Alps."

At the station we met the train going in the opposite direction that was only nine hours late, and I chatted with Vice-President Hanna of the Canadian Northern whose story I later told you. He had come to Canada as poor as a church mouse and had become the buyer for the railway. During a short trip in Quebec, the train ran over a cow whose owner at once demanded compensation. Hanna bargained for $25.00 and went back into the car supposedly to get the money. In the train with Hanna travelled the supplier of groceries and Hanna quickly sold him the dead cow for $50.00. After this ingenious trick, Hanna's future was secured and now he is a multi-millionaire.

At the Pacific Ocean

After a short stay, we continued our trip along the beautiful Shuswap Lakes that are so similar to the Bavarian lakes, slowly descended to North Bend and reached the Pacific Ocean in Vancouver. You were not just a little proud to be interviewed in the hotel by a newspaper reporter who had heard about our ride. When you read about your heroic deeds in the paper the next day, you must have acquired far too much self-esteem. Do not always believe the pleasant things people tell you; they more readily will tell the truth about unpleasant things.

VANCOUVER, B. C., SATURDAY MORNING, SEPTEMBER 28, 1912—SIXTEEN P

Little Miss Here From Thrilling Trip

* * * * * * * *   * * * * * * * *

First Woman Over Pipe Stem Pass

Arriving last evening at the Vancouver hotel, charming little Miss Nordegg, daughter of Herr Martin Nordegg, a German capitalist of Nuremburg, recounted to a Sun reporter the story of her thrilling trip across the Pipe Stem pass in the Rocky mountains, a route never previously traversed by a white woman.

The trip was made over a range of mountains about which many weird tales are related. Prospectors and miners threading their way upon the unmarked paths and mountainous barren peaks have been frequently hurled to death and destruction by the force of the storm king's wrath. Dangerous blizzards rage almost continually at the highest points along the pass and the trail is perpetually wrapped in a cold, dank veil of wraith-like clouds.

Miss Nordegg's trip was made in company with her father, two cowboys and a couple of Indian guides. Starting on the second day of September from the town or Nordegg, situated on the eastern slope of the Rockies, the party followed along the shores of the Saskatchewan river until the junction of the Big Horn river was reached, where a fording was effffected. From thence the coterie of guides led the way up the Siffleur over the Pipe Stem pass and down the Pipe Stem river, coming out at Laggan.

Ten hours daily in the saddle, an exhausting feat even for the hardy rider of the plains, was the feat accomplished by Miss Nordegg. At an altitude of 8,400 feet blinding sleet storms and blizzards were encountered that threatened . at times sweep the party from their pracarious footing upon the narrow and devious trails that wind spirally along the faces of the weather-beaten cliffs. The little Fraulein withstood the strenuous onslaught of the elements and arrived in Laggan with the flush upon her cheeks that only the wind-swept vastness of the Rockies can bring.

"Were you not the littlest bit frightened at the danger and the storms?" curiously queried the reporter as Miss Nordegg finished her story.

"Just once, when the horse stumbled and I lost my hat over a 1000-foot cliff," smiled the girl as she concluded the interview.

Later, we took a steamboat to Victoria and Seattle and then travelled by train five nights and four days back to Toronto. A short time later, we started on the big trip from New York via the Azores, Gibraltar, Palermo and Naples to Genoa where you were happy to embrace your beloved mother after months of separation.

The trip half around the world — from the Pacific Ocean to the shores of the Mediterranean Sea — had ended. You had travelled the long rail and ocean journeys so often that they hardly offered anything new to you. But on this trip, you took part in the strenuous ride into the wilderness, your eyes viewed the wonders of the lonely mountains, you learned to bear tiredness without complaining, to be satisfied with the simplest food and to try out the spice of hunger after heavy physical effort, to let the "categorical imperative" affect your, at times, quite rebellious mind, to subordinate your will to the discipline of the packtrain, to wrap your blankets around you in the evenings without missing the soft bed, to weather dangers without batting an eyelash and, last but not least, to have to depend on your own resources and not on others. All this, I hope, my dear child, made an indelible impression upon you. You learned to overcome pain and discomfort in silence and you demonstrated that you, a child still young, could bear what strong men shy away from, only because they lack willpower and energy.

And when years later, these pages and pictures come to your attention again, then let all of us who enjoyed your company come to life again — the stoical Indians, the prudent Stuart, the cheerful Tom and, last but not least, the one who loves you so much, your

Father.

Martin Nordegg

Nordegg soon after World War I (Courtesy of the Nordegg Historical Society).

Nordegg as viewed from the north west (Courtesy of the Nordegg Historical Society).

EPILOGUE

Why did Martin Nordegg decide to meet his wife in Genoa rather than in Hamburg, Bremen or Rotterdam, his usual ports of arrival?

After the adventurous journey with her father, Marcelle was anxious to be re-united with her mother. Worry about her mother had been the only cloud that had thrown a shadow on her wonderful experience of crossing Canada with her father. Longing for her mother, mentioned several times in Martin's story, was more than the result of Marcelle's separation from her mother. Berthe-Marie had been seriously ill for several years.

Rather than returning to Germany from Genoa, Marcelle travelled to another foreign land instead, to accompany her mother to Egypt, to the resort of Helouan, famous among the well-to-do of Europe for its clean, dry desert air, where Marcelle's mother hoped to find relief, perhaps even cure of her chronic lung ailment.

After attending to his business affairs in Germany and England, Martin returned to Alberta where the coal mine and the town named after him were nearing completion.

On a bright, sunny day in March 1914, the official train carrying the dignitaries of the Canadian Northern Railway stopped in front of the new station building in Nordegg. While the guests alighted from the special car, Martin remained on its rear platform, his eyes gazing towards his town and its mine. A photograph taken at this memorable moment shows Martin in the proud pose of the victor, the general inspecting his accomplishments.

What Martin viewed with great satisfaction was a charming town imbedded in the beautiful foothills country at the entrance to the Rocky Mountains, a town where new houses were still springing up along the crescents laid out on the vast slope rising towards the hills behind the town. (See back cover for town plan). Much thought had gone into the town plan, modeled after the Mount Royal district in Montreal which had been developed by the Canadian Northern Railway a few years earlier. The designs for both Mount Royal and Nordegg had their origin in the English garden cities planned by Ebenezer Howard around London towards the end of the nineteenth century. Martin himself had lived in one of these garden cities during the first years of his marriage.

Nordegg did not only carry Martin's name,* it was his town with several streets and lanes named after people dear to him. He named the most prominent residential street after his daughter Marcelle. Other streets were named after his trusted friends Stuart Kidd, Ernest Gheur, the Belgian consulting engineer, and Gheur's wife Marthe. He named another Cherie Street, likely after his first wife, who was French-born.

Nordegg was a town offering its residents amenities far in excess of anything known in the West and, indeed, in most mining towns throughout North America. It was Martin's intention to provide a working and living environment for his miners and their families that was to be pleasant, dignified and promoting a harmonious way of life in exchange for

---

* The Nordegg River, a tributary of the Blackstone River, and Martin Creek at the edge of Nordegg are both named in honour of Martin Nordegg.

their loyalty to their employer. That ideal probably came closer to reality in Nordegg than anywhere in Alberta. Indeed, Nordegg remained the only planned company town in the province and, throughout its lifetime, was remarkably free of labour strife and unrest.

Above the town, slightly to the west, rose the buildings of Martin's mine, later called the Brazeau Collieries. Soon, the mine would become one of Alberta's most modern coal mining operations. Close to the end of the tracks, a very proud and satisfied Martin Nordegg saw the huge piles of coal — over one hundred thousand tons of it — ready for shipment as soon as the railway reached the minehead, as he had promised his partner Sir William Mackenzie.

On this unforgettable day and for a few months after, Martin cherished the feeling that he had reached the zenith of his life. But, he had many more plans. They included planting alpine gardens with plants he had imported from Switzerland, opening facilities for tourists, more coalfields, and building his home — a Swiss chalet on the shore of the little reservoir, nestled in the forest above the town. Four months later, World War I broke out, an event which irreversibly changed Martin's plans for his town and his mine.

Although technically an "enemy alien," Martin was permitted to remain in Nordegg and continue his work until June 1915, when the Dominion government called him to Ottawa and suggested that, until the end of hostilities, he take up residence in the United States. He was issued a special passport, however, which permitted him to cross the international boundary without difficulty as he did on many occasions.

Spending the remaining years of World War I with his wife and daughter in New York City and Atlantic City, Martin eagerly awaited his permanent return to Canada. In April 1918, seven months before the end of the war, his wife and daughter travelled, by special permission of the U.S. government, to China where Marcelle married an American citizen.

Remaining in New York City, Martin watched with mounting anxiety the developments in Canada that, for several reasons, some of them connected to the war and its outcome, led to his eventual removal from his positions as vice-president, director and manager of the Brazeau Collieries.

In 1924, Martin Nordegg's wife Berthe-Marie, ill for many years, died in Switzerland. Shortly after, Martin Nordegg re-married entering into a happy and rewarding relationship with his second wife Sonia. Sonia had come from Russian Poland to New York with her parents as a young woman in 1904. Soon after, she became a well-known actress on the stages of New York, Chicago, and Atlantic City. She also appeared on the silent screen.

Meanwhile, an unhappy Marcelle, who had given birth to a son in 1919, divorced her husband and returned to Germany, leaving her little son behind in China.

Before returning to Canada in 1920, Martin had already offered his services to the government and the Liberal Party of Canada. He provided advice and consultation in international trade and finance matters and received various assignments from the

Canadian government. In 1929, he and Sonia took up residence on Range Road, then Ottawa's embassy row. Their home became a social centre in Ottawa, frequently used by Prime Minister Mackenzie King for entertaining his guests from foreign countries.

During the later 1930s, Martin and Sonia offered advice, support and financial help to hundreds of refugees from Hitler's Germany. Only days after Hitler's annexation of Austria, Martin hurried to Vienna, at great personal risk and against the explicit advice of the British ambassador in Prague, to help some of his friends and their families escape from threatened imprisonment and persecution. These humanitarian efforts continued after the Nordeggs moved back to New York at the beginning of World War II. They extended their help to war victims, orphaned children and numerous other people in need.

During the inter-war years, Martin and Sonia had travelled throughout the world collecting art treasures that now filled their apartment at Central Park West in New York City. Only once more, since his forced departure from Brazeau Collieries, did Martin return to his beloved Nordegg in 1927. He and Sonia lived in the cottage of his old friend Dutchie in Harlech, eight miles east of Nordegg. Martin still hoped to regain a foothold in the area by opening another mining venture at Harlech with his old friends Stuart Kidd and Dutchie, but their efforts did not come to fruition.

In the meantime, Nordegg and its mine experienced the vagaries of time, as production of coal always depended on the needs of the market. Its labour force reached its highest point of 800 mine workers in 1923, while the population of the town reportedly came close to 2000 persons. Altogether, during its lifetime of forty-two years, the Brazeau Collieries produced over 10,000,000 tons of coal.

Two disasters hit the mine and the people of the town. An explosion in 1941, killed 29 miners, and, in 1951, fire destroyed the briquette plant. A new, more modern and larger briquette plant was built immediately, the second largest of its kind in North America, but the declining use of coal, largely the result of the change to diesel power by Canada's railways, caused the permanent closure of the mine and the town in 1955.

After years of neglect and vandalism, the mine and town were finally protected by the Alberta government. However, most of the town was razed and the mine buildings continued to crumble. In 1984 a group of interested citizens formed the Nordegg Historical Interest Society. It was renamed the Nordegg Historical Society in 1994, when the mine site was declared a Provincial Historical Site by the Government of Alberta. Much work has been done and more plans are being made by the Nordegg Historical Society to protect, preserve and, where feasible, restore what has survived the ravages of time. A museum preserves the history of Nordegg and its people. Old-timers and their descendants still meet for a camp-out in Nordegg every year in August.

Martin never knew about the sad end of his beloved town. In 1938, much encouraged by his wife, he had written an account of his Canadian years, *The Possibilities of Canada Are Truly Great.* It was never published in its original form. In

October 1945, he learned that his daughter Marcelle, who had been a patient in a private psychiatric clinic in Bonn, Germany since 1931, had died in January 1945, three months before the end of World War II. It was strongly suspected that she had been murdered by the authorities of that day.

Depressed and ill towards the end of his life, Martin Nordegg still wanted to see his town once more. Faithfully, he had maintained his friendship with Stuart Kidd and Tom Wilson and Dutchie over the years. But Stuart had retired from his position as manager of the Bighorn Trading Company in Nordegg and had moved to Edmonton, Tom Wilson now lived in Calgary, and Dutchie had left Harlech for a few weeks of travel never to return. Martin and Sonia made reservations at Jasper Park Lodge for the summer of 1948, but Martin's rapidly declining health forced him to cancel the visit.

Martin Norgegg died in New York City in September 1948, at the age of 80. His wife Sonia survived him by almost 22 years. She died in New York in May 1970.

In Bonn, the mass grave, where Marcelle Nordegg-May was buried in January 1945, has since been levelled and can no longer be found.

W. John Koch

The Nordeggs in the 1930s

Sonia Nordegg   Martin Nordegg*

Sonia and Marcelle

---

* Courtesy of the National Archives of Canada

BIOGRAPHIES

Maria Koch was born Maria Schuster in Saxony, Germany. After World War II, Saxony was part of the German Democratic Republic which she was forced to leave in 1948.

Maria studied and graduated at the University of Würzburg in West Germany and taught high school there until her emigration to Canada in 1957 where she married John Koch. For the next few years, she worked in social welfare in Saskatchewan and British Columbia. In 1964, she resumed her teaching career as a lecturer of German at the University of Alberta where she taught for 27 years until her retirement.

Maria and John have a son, George, who works as a free-lance journalist in Calgary.

John Koch was born in Silesia, the German province where Martin Nordegg was born in 1868.

Following World War II, John attended the University of Würzburg before emigrating to Canada in 1954. After further studies at the University of British Columbia where he obtained a masters degree in social work in 1960, John worked in the social welfare and health-care fields in the provinces of British Columbia, Saskatchewan and, since 1964, Alberta. John retired in 1987.

John published several articles in professional journals and other social and health care publications in Canada, the United States and Poland. He is the author of *Schloss Fürstenstein,* an illustrated volume about a famous German castle, since 1945 in Poland, and of the biography of the *Princess Daisy of Pless,* both books published in Germany in 1989 and 1991 respectively. John Koch is currently preparing a biography of Martin Nordegg and welcomes any documentation or personal memories. He and his wife Maria have been residents of Edmonton since 1964.

First train at Nordegg Mine. Martin standing on platform. Courtesy of the Red Deer Archives, Fleming Collection

Brazeau Collieries in the 1920s. Courtesy of the Nordegg Historical Society